88751

629.2
Bur

D0576820

THE
ILLUSTRATED HISTORY OF
ROAD
TRANSPORT

THE
ILLUSTRATED HISTORY OF
ROAD
TRANSPORT

DAVID BURGESS-WISE

DENIS MILLER

ERWIN TRAGATSCH

Automobiles
Phototypeset in England by Filmtype Service Ltd.
Colour separation by Sakai Lithocolour

Trucks & Buses
Typeset by Everbest Printing Company Ltd.
Colour separations by Rodney Howe, England

Motorcycles
Phototypeset in England by Filmtype Services
Colour separation by Sakai Lithocolour

This book was designed and produced by Quarto
Publishing Limited, 6 Blundell St, London N.7.

Printed by Leefung-Asco Printers Limited,
Hong Kong

ISBN 0-948872-12-8

Published by New Burlington Books.

1936 Auburn 852 supercharged cabriolet

Contents

AUTOMOBILES

DAVID BURGESS-WISE

Prehistory

MAN'S SEARCH FOR some form of motive power to replace the horse goes back over 300 years; clockwork, wind power and elaborate clockwork gearing were all tried before the power of steam became tractable enough to be used to drive a vehicle. Not that it was initially too successful: the oldest surviving self-propelled vehicle, Cugnot's 1770 *fardier*, owes its preservation to the fact that on its trial runs it ran amok and knocked down a wall! Put into store, it survived the French Revolution, was acquired by the Conservatoire des Arts et Métiers in Paris in 1799, and has been a major exhibit there ever since.

It was followed by a number of even less practical designs from optimistic French, English and American engineers, and it was not until 1801 that the first successful road carriage appeared. This was the work of the Cornish mining engineer Richard Trevithick and led to his London Carriage of 1803, which made a number of successful runs in the capital before it was dismantled to power a hoop rolling mill. Trevithick lacked the staying power to perfect either this or his other great invention, the railway carriage. He was succeeded by a lunatic gaggle of inventors who proposed machines driven by articulated legs, tiny railway engines running inside a drum like squirrels, compressed air, gunpowder and 'vanes, or fliers, like the sails of a windmill'.

Then, between 1820 and 1840, came a golden age of steam, with skilled engineers devising and operating steam carriages of advanced and ingenious design; men like Gurney, Hancock and Macerone all produced designs which were practicable, capable of achieving quite lengthy journeys and operating with a relatively high degree of reliability. Walter Hancock, a better mechanic than businessman, operated his steam coaches on regular scheduled services in London in the 1830s, but was rooked by his associates, and eventually called it a day after 12 years of experiment had brought him little more than unpaid debts and the hostility of those with vested interests, who, fearing that the steam carriage would prove a threat to the thousands whose livelihood depended on the horse, promoted swingeing tolls on the turnpike roads; an 1831 Parliamentary Commission, though largely favourable to the steam carriage, failed to prevent such injustices, and the final blow to the builders of steam carriages came with the advent of the railway age. Railway engines, running on smooth, level rails, had none of the problems experienced by steam carriages running on uneven, badly maintained roads, and this newer form of locomotion soon eclipsed the steam carriage, even though legislation restricting the speed and operation of steam carriages was not enacted until 1863, when it was decreed that all 'road locomotives' should have a man with a red flag walking ahead.

It was the advent of the bicycle in the 1860s which revived touring by road.

Some of the successes and failures of the prehistory of motoring: James's steam carriage (**1**) was one of the better road carriages of the early 1830s, while Dr Church's Birmingham Road Carriage (**2**) was never completed in this baroque style. The 1770 Cugnot (**3**) is the world's oldest self-propelled vehicle to survive, though it is possible that it never ran. Johann Hautsch of Nürnberg devised this curious clockwork carriage (**4**) in the seventeenth century, while the Hancock steam drag of c.1830 (**5**) represents the high point of early British steam carriages.

Radiators

The earliest cars, which, if they even had radiators to cool their engines, had them slung at the rear of the chassis or some other anatomically improbable position, lacked a certain amount of character. When, however, Mercedes developed the honeycomb radiator into a recognizable marque symbol, cars began to acquire personality. And, despite the hiding of the radiator behind a grille, it is still front end treatment that gives a car its character.

When Ettore Bugatti originally adopted a shape for the radiators of his cars (1), he apparently followed the outline of a chairback designed by his furniture-designer father, Carlo. The 1949 Bristol 400 (2) took its functional radiator openings from the BMW with which it was closely connected. Typical of its era, the 1913 Unic radiator (3) reflects honest craftsmanship, while the flamboyant frontal treatment of the 1959 Ford Fairlane Skyliner (4) is a product of a time when the stylist was king. On the other hand, the 1936 Railton (5) cloaked its American origins behind a very English radiator.

6

7

8

10

Like an Art Deco fencer's mask, the radiator grill of the 1936 Triumph Dolomite (**6**) is one of the more extreme designs of a decade when styling began to influence sales. But the crude front end of the 1921 Carden cyclecar (**7**) is purely a dummy, aping larger cars. The 'dollar grin' of the 1947 Buick Eight (**8**) celebrates an age of promise (of increased sales!) after World War Two; over 20 years on, a new era of restraint is marked by the bland front end of the 1970 Monteverdi 375L (**9**). The Rolls-Royce radiator (**10**) has remained true to its original design concept for over 75 years.

1880 to 1900

THE INTERNAL COMBUSTION engine appeared early in the history of the motor vehicle, but took over three-quarters of a century to be perfected to the level where it could be used in a vehicle capable of running on the roads—the 1805 powered cart of the Swiss Isaac de Rivaz was no more than an elaborate toy, only capable of crawling from one side of a room to another, and the 1863 car built in Paris by J-J. Etienne Lenoir took three hours to cover six miles. It was not until the mid-1880s that the first successful petrol cars appeared, developed independently by two German engineers, Gottlieb Daimler and Karl Benz.

Of the two vehicles, that of Benz was incontestably superior, for it was designed as an entity, using the new technology of the cycle industry, while Daimler's carriage was no more than an adapted horse vehicle. Benz went into limited production of his three-wheeled carriages (described in his catalogue as 'an agreeable vehicle, as well as a mountain-climbing apparatus') in 1888; Daimler was more interested in selling his engines as a universal power source.

Neither man found immediate success, but neither had the great geniuses of the steam vehicle who were their contemporaries. The Bollée family of Le Mans built some truly advanced steam carriages between 1873 and the mid-1880s, vehicles which pioneered independent front suspension, while blacksmith's son Léon Serpollet conceived the 'flash boiler' for instantaneous generation of steam and held the first driving licence issued in Paris. And while the Comte De Dion and his engineers Bouton and Trépardoux built some excellent steam vehicles during the 1880s and early 1890s, they were to achieve their greatest fame as manufacturers of light petrol vehicles, from 1895 on.

The crucial event in the story of the motor car was the 1889 Paris World Exhibition, for it was there that the French engineers Panhard and Levassor saw the Daimler 'Steelwheeler' car powered by the Daimler vee-twin engine. Levassor's lady friend, an astute widow named Louise Sarazin, held the French rights to the Daimler engine in succession to her late husband, and Panhard and Levassor began manufacturing these power units in 1890. They could, however, see no future for the motor car, and so granted the right to use Daimler engines in self-propelled vehicles to the ironmongery and cycle firm of Peugeot (who had just decided not to go ahead with the planned production of Serpollet steamers).

It was in France, too, that Benz enjoyed his first limited success, for his Paris agent, Emile Roger, managed to sell one or two Benz cars in Paris (and, coincidentally, garaged his first Benz in Panhard and Levassor's workshop). But it was not until his first four-wheeler, the 1893 Viktoria, that Benz began series production.

Peugeot were already established as motor manufacturers by that date, for in 1891 they had

De Dion, Bouton and Trépardoux built this neat little steam car in 1885 (**1**); the lordly Bollée *Mancelle* steam carriage of 1873 (**2**) was a precursor of petrol car design, with the engine under a frontal bonnet driving the rear wheels, and independent front suspension. Indeed, the 1899 Fiat 3½hp (**3**) and its contemporaries were far more primitive in concept. The first petrol car conceived as an entity was the 1885–86 Benz three-wheeler (**4**). Serpollet's 1888 three-wheeler (**5**) used his high-speed flash boiler. The 1895 tricar (**6**) utilized the power unit from a Leyland steam lawnmower.

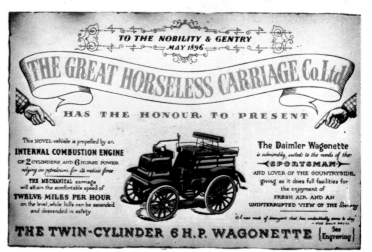

Couched in glowing Victorian prose, this advertisement (**left**) is, in fact, a pastiche conceived for Daimler's 40th anniversary in 1936! Built by a firm once famed for sewing machines and cycles, the 1898 Hurtu (**below**) (whose name did nothing to recommend the marque to timorous English motorists!) is a typical horseless carriage.

actually sold 5 cars, boosting production to a dizzy 29 the following year.

The success of the Peugeot cars inspired Panhard and Levassor to reconsider their early opinion of the horseless carriage, and, after building a couple of crude dogcarts with the engine at the rear, Levassor devised the famous *Système Panhard*, with the engine at the front driving the rear wheels via a sliding pinion gearbox inspired by the mechanism of a lathe, a layout which, however '*brusque et brutale*' its inventor thought it, has been used on the majority of motor cars built since.

In America, the motor car was evolving along different lines from Europe and, in January-February 1891, the New World's first petrol vehicle, a friction-driven three-wheeler built by John W. Lambert of Ohio City, made its first tentative runs. In 1895, America's first motor manufacturing company was founded by the Duryea brothers, Charles and Frank (whose prototype dated from 1893); the following year they exported a couple of vehicles to Britain. However, anti-motoring prejudice in that country was running high, and there was little encouragement for motor vehicles, either home-grown or imported (though the company promotions of the so-called 'father of the British motor industry', H. J. Lawson, succeeded in parting a good many credulous investors from a large amount of cash).

Lawson had influential friends and in 1896 succeeded in getting the ridiculous requirement for motor cars to be preceded by a man on foot (a legacy of the old Locomotives on Highways Acts of 1865 and 1878) to be repealed, and held a commemorative run to Brighton on November 14, 1896 to celebrate the raising of the speed limit to 12 mph. Some of the participating machines, though, covered the distance by train and were cosmetically muddied after they had been unloaded, and the first machine home, a Duryea, was not one of the marques under Lawson's aegis (he had expensively purchased a great number of motor car patents in a forlorn effort to monopolize the nascent British car industry).

Demand for motor cars was growing steadily during the latter part of the 1890s, and by now the Benz had become the world's most popular car, with the 2000th production vehicle being delivered in 1899. Motoring was still the sport of a few rich eccentrics, however, and many people had never seen a car.

It was to remedy this defect that, in 1900, the Automobile Club of Great Britain and Ireland held its famous 1000 Miles Trial, which took in most of the major cities of England and Scotland. A total of 65 cars, many English Daimler and MMC models built by Lawson's empire, set out from Hyde Park Corner, London, in April; the major part of this entry finished the run without major mishap, proving that the motor car had at last become a reliable—or relatively so — touring vehicle after a century's gestation.

Badges and mascots

Radiator badges were the heraldry of the early motor car. Starting as simply makers' plates fixed to the radiator, badges quickly developed into a minor art form. Some badges, indeed, were masterpieces of the enameller's craft; the Invicta was endowed with a polychromatic butterfly badge delicate enough for jewellery. As for mascots, they began as good luck charms like teddy bears tied to the radiator, but soon the techniques of statuary were being employed to produce mascots of real beauty. The Hispano stork and the Rolls-Royce 'Spirit of Ecstasy' became marque symbols, though owners also commissioned individual mascots, like the Wagnerian soprano whose Métallurgique was endowed with a sterling silver Seigfried clad in chain mail.

(1) The Calometer temperature gauge, a popular 1920s accessory, on a 1927 Morris-Cowley. (2) Packard's emblem – 'a pelican in her piety'. (3) A one-off mascot on a Cadillac V-8. (4) The Hotchkiss badge recalls the firm's origin. (5) A 1914 Star 15.9hp. (6) Jaguar's mascot, derived from a sculpture by motoring artist Gordon Crosby. (7) The Armstrong Siddeley sphinx.

1901 to 1914

THE NEW CENTURY was spectacularly ushered in by 'the car of the day after tomorrow', the Mercedes, designed by Daimler's engineer, Wilhelm Maybach. The contract to produce the first batch of 30 cars had been signed within a month of Gottlieb Daimler's death in March 1900. They had been ordered by the wealthy Austro-Hungarian Consul at Nice, Emil Jellinek, who insisted that they be christened after his daughter Mercédès, a name which found such favour with the wealthy car-buying public that all German Daimler cars were soon known as 'Mercedes', too.

The advanced design of the Mercedes, which combined in one harmonious whole elements such as the honeycomb radiator, pressed steel chassis and gear-lever moving in a gate rather than a quadrant, 'set the fashion to the world' and soon many high-priced cars were copying its layout; even comparatively small cars like the Peugeot were built on Mercedes lines.

These cars did not, however, represent the 'popular motoring' of the early 1900s; this was the province of single-cylinder runabouts like the De Dion and the Renault—again, these well-built cars were widely imitated—and, in America, first by light and temperamental steam cars like the Locomobile and then by gas buggies, of which the most famous was the Curved-Dash Oldsmobile.

But the development of the motor industry in America was being hampered—as it had in Britain a few years earlier—by the shadow of monopoly. A patent lawyer named George Baldwin Selden had drawn up a 'master patent' for the motor vehicle in 1879, published it in 1895 and claimed that all gasoline-driven vehicles were infringements of that patent. His claims were eventually given commercial teeth by the Association of Licenced Automobile Manufacturers, established to administer the Selden Patent in 1902, to which most major American car firms were persuaded to belong.

However, Henry Ford, who founded his Ford Motor Company in June 1903, decided to stand against the ALAM, who began proceedings against him in 1904. After lengthy litigation, which resulted in the ALAM building a car to Selden's 1879 design and Ford building a car with an engine based on that of the 1863 Lenoir, Ford won the day in 1911—not long before the Selden Patent would have expired anyway—but the victory established him as a folk hero.

Ford's great achievement, after five years' work, was to introduce in October 1908 the immortal Model T, which became so popular that he was forced to introduce the car industry's first moving production line in order to build enough cars to satisfy demand. His 'Universal Car' changed the face of motoring; over 16·5 million were built before production ended in 1927, truly 'putting the world on wheels' and transforming the face of society.

A 1901 Curved-Dash Oldsmobile

Though the Edwardian era saw motoring become more popular, on the other hand it also saw the finest and most elegant cars of all time, built to a standard of craftsmanship which could never be repeated. After World War One, many of the great marques faded away in a genteel decline: Delaunay-Belleville, 'the Car Magnificent', the favourite marque of the Tsar of Russia and one of the very best of the French cars of the pre-1914 era, became just a *petit bourgeois* in the 1920s.

Napier, the British company which popularized the six-cylinder engine, enjoyed perhaps even greater acclaim than its rival, Rolls-Royce, while its sales were controlled by that bombastic character Selwyn Francis Edge; when Napier gave him a £160,000 'golden handshake' after a dispute over policy in 1912, however, the company's fortunes seemed to leave with him. Edge, having agreed to leave the motor industry for seven years, became a successful Sussex pig-farmer; Napier built very few cars after the war, concentrating instead on its aero engines.

Such ostentatious machinery relied for its existence on a pool of highly skilled, lowly paid craftsmen with a surpassing pride in their work; against the onslaught of cheap machines produced in America by unskilled labour using production techniques which eliminated most of the human factor, the big luxury cars stood little chance. They represented only a tiny fraction of the potential market for the motor vehicle and, even if their production had not been decimated by the drying up of the car market as a result of the war, they would inevitably have died out as a result of the social changes in the post-war world.

Europe, indeed, experienced an outburst of popular motoring in the 1910–14 period which owed nothing to American concepts of mass production; instead, it grew out of the motor-cycle industry, whose engines, single-cylinder or vee-twin, offered lightness and power. Optimistic enthusiasts installed these engines in chassis of often suicidal crudeness, with cart-type centre-pivot steering in many cases, as well as other unmechanical devices such as wire cables coiled round the steering column instead of a conventional steering box and drag link, belt and pulley transmission and tandem-seat layouts with the driver in the second row of the stalls. These crude devices, known as cyclecars, flourished especially in England and France; attempts to transplant them to America failed because they were simply unsuited to the very different motoring environment there.

The worst of the cyclecars were short-lived, however; the designs of the late Edwardian period which promised perhaps the most for the future were the new light cars like the Morris-Oxford, the Standard and the Hillman, all 'big cars in miniature' of around 1100cc, with four cylinders and built on proper engineering lines. These admirable machines were to be the pattern for the popular family cars of the 1920s.

One of the great names of motoring in the Edwardian era was Napier: this 1907 60hp six-cylinder (1) has been constructed as a replica of the car on which S. F. Edge averaged over 60mph for 24 hours to inaugurate the Brooklands race track. This 1903 Fiat 16/20hp (2) was shown at the Agricultural Hall Exhibition in London: its Grosvenor tonneau body is English-built. The popular impression that motor cars were 'engines of death' is illustrated by this 1904 cartoon (3); a more idealized concept of motoring is shown in the 1908 Argyll advertisement (4).

Another, if humbler, 'immortal' of the period was the twin-cylinder Renault AX (**5**), for this chassis was used on the taxis which ferried troops to the Battle of the Marne and saved Paris in 1914. Some of the ignorant fear of motoring may have been caused by the strange garb affected by early motorists, like these sinister anti-dust masks (**6**), from 1907.

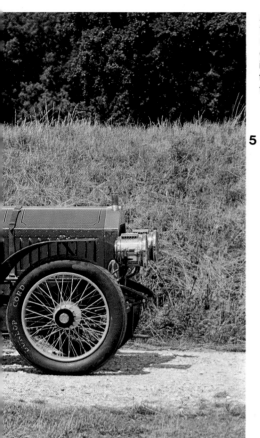

5

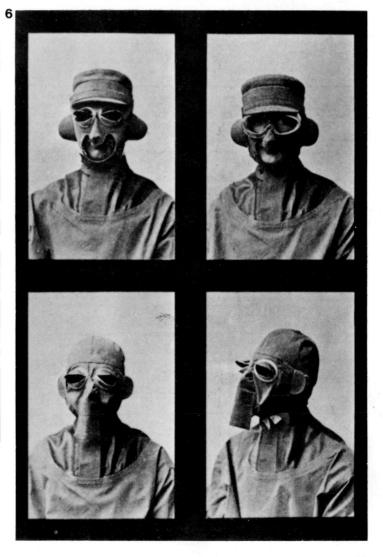

6

4

Wheels

The wheel is one of man's most fundamental inventions, as it has no parallel in nature. The earliest cars rolled into the world on wire wheels derived from cycle practice, or on wooden wheels developed from those used on carriages. These basic types have been followed by many different patterns of wheel: only the roundness has remained constant.

The wire wheels of the 1898 Hurtu (1) are typical of those used on many early light cars. Their spindly construction makes them unsuitable for high speed. One of the odder inventions of Edwardian times was this hub-mounted tyre pump (2), here fitted to a wooden-wheeled Gladiator. Wooden artillery wheels (3) were common on most pre-World War One European cars, and were still being used in America throughout the 1920s. Bugatti's famous spoked aluminium wheels (4) were developed for racing use. Cheap to make and light in weight, they could be changed complete with brake drum.

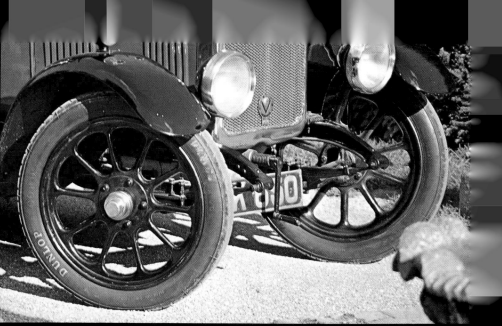

The spokes on the wheels of this Model A Ford (**5**) are electrically welded to the rim, not located by adjustable nipples as on conventional wire wheels. The wheels on this 1923 Calcott (**6**) are pressed steel simulating wooden artillery wheels, a popular fashion on British light cars of the 1920s. Wheeltrims have ranged from vulgar (**7**) to the elegantly practical (**8**), the latter being used to protect a wire-spoked wheel and make it easier to clean. Styling of wheels is nothing new – compare the Bugatti of the 1930s (**9**) with the Alfasud (**10**)

1915 to 1930

THE TECHNOLOGY of the motor age revolutionized the way that World War One was fought. The internal combustion engine gave new mobility to the infantry who, before hostilities in Europe came to a standstill in the trenches, could be rushed to reinforce weak points in the front line (most notably when the French General Gallieni sent 6000 reinforcements to repel Von Kluck's attack on Paris in 1914); it also provided motorcycles for despatch riders, permitted H. G. Wells's forecast of 'land ironclads' to be fulfilled in the angular shapes of the first armoured cars and tanks and, perhaps most significantly, gave warfare a new dimension by taking it into the air.

One way and another, most of those who fought in the war were given an insight into the utility of the motor vehicle, and when peace came many returning soldiers were only too anxious to spend their demobilization pay on a car of their own. The result was a boom such as the motor industry had never known. Especially in Britain and France, the established manufacturers found themselves contending for the favours of the car-buying public with a whole new sub-industry of optimists who, working from inadequate back-street premises, assembled light cars and cyclecars from proprietary components in the hope that they might make their fortunes. Most found only commercial failure, like the British firm who, with the bailiffs mounting a 24-hour watch outside the doors of their London factory, broke an exit through the unguarded rear wall, loaded as much of their machinery as possible on to the finished chassis and drove off to seek new (but unforthcoming) fortune in the Midlands.

If the American industry had already developed to the extent where success in popular car sales would inevitably go to the established big battalions (even Chrysler, founded in 1924, sprang from the established Maxwell-Briscoe grouping), there was still room in Europe for new mass-producers. Most spectacular of these was André Citroën, a former gear manufacturer, who, with the aim of bringing Ford-style mass-production to France, enjoyed an immediate success with his 10 hp launched in 1919. However, the rise of Citroën spelt doom for the dozens of optimistic assemblers who clustered most thickly in the north-western suburbs of Paris.

The boom collapsed in 1920–21, speeded on its way by strikes, hold-ups, shortages, loss of stock market confidence in the car industry, restrictions on hire-purchase sales, costlier raw materials, and the introduction of a swingeing horsepower tax in Britain.

Only the fittest survived: Ford, whose example was followed by a number of American and European makers, cut prices in order to boost falling sales (though he compensated for

The Blackhawk of 1929 was a short-lived attempt by Stutz to build a lower-priced car.

the loss on the cars by compelling the dealers to take $40-worth of spare parts on which there had been no reduction) and gained a brief respite, though even he had to close down for some months to clear unsold stocks. It was not until 1922 that the motor industry was back on course and a second generation of post-war popular cars began to emerge, most notably the Austin Seven.

Many of the cars of the 1920s profited from the technology of the aero engines developed during the war, most notably the overhead camshaft Hispano-Suiza V-8. Wolseley built this engine under licence and used an overhead camshaft on their post-war cars, but it was not until after the 1927 takeover by Morris that this Wolseley design realized its full potential, especially in MG sports cars.

Hispano-Suiza put their aero engine expertise to full account in the 1919 32cv of 6·6 litres, a splendid machine with servo-assisted four-wheel brakes and delightful handling characteristics, whose overall conception was several years ahead of any of its rivals.

Bentley, who had built rotary aero engines during the war, brought out an in-line four with an overhead camshaft in 1919 (though it was not put into production until 1921); this 3-litre was to become one of the immortal sporting cars.

Many leading manufacturers adopted the overhead camshaft layout during this period, but Rolls-Royce, whose aero engines had used this layout, stuck resolutely to side valves on their cars until the advent of the 20 in 1922; this had pushrod ohv, a configuration followed on the 1925 Phantom which was to supplant the Silver Ghost, which had side valves till the end.

Oddly enough, apart from honourable exceptions like the Hispano, it was the cheaper cars which pioneered the use of brakes on all four wheels, one of the most positive advances in car equipment in the early 1920s. Possibly it was felt that luxury cars would be handled by professional drivers, who would be less likely to indulge in the kind of reckless driving that would require powerful brakes! Moreover, some American popular car makers, appalled at the cost of retooling their cars to accept brakes on the front wheels, actually campaigned against their introduction on the grounds that they were dangerous.

As the decade wore on, more features designed to make motoring more comfortable and safer became commonplace—windscreen wipers, electric starters, safety glass (first standardized on the 1928 Model A Ford), all-steel coachwork, saloon bodies, low-pressure tyres, cellulose paint and chromium plating all became available on popular cars. Styling and the annual model change became an accepted part of the selling of motor cars, bringing with them huge tooling costs which could only be borne by the biggest companies. Many old-established firms just could not keep up and were swept away by the onslaught of the depression in 1929.

Typical of American quality car design in the late 1920s is this 1929 Packard 640 six-cylinder phaeton (**1**). The Hispano H6B (**2**) was one of the great designs of the 1920s. A 1925 aluminium-bodied sports version of the 10.8hp Riley (**3**), normally known as the 'Redwinger'. Two of the most famous popular cars of the era were the Morris-Cowley 'Bullnose' (**4**) and the Model T Ford (**5**). Their very different designs reflect popular taste in Britain and America.

Body styles

Since the dawn of motoring, a bewildering lexicon of words has been used to describe automobile bodywork, many descending from horse-carriage practice, others coined by car manufacturers. Some became standard practice, like the use of the word 'torpedo' to describe an open four-seater touring car; others, like the similar 'gunboat roadster', vanished into limbo. Fashion, too, has played its part in determining names: in America, 'touring' was superseded by 'phaeton' in an attempt to standardize coachwork nomenclature. And, of course, there are the national differences in usage – a 'saloon' is a closed car in England, a public bar in America, where the car becomes a 'sedan'. Henry Ford devised the names 'Tudor' (two-door) and 'Fordor' (four-door) to describe the Model T sedan; after more than 50 years these names are still in use internally in the Ford Motor Company. Today, there is little variation in body styles – most cars are saloons, though 'hatchback' and 'notchback' are specialized subdivisions of the type. Legislation has all but killed off the convertible, save for specialist sports cars, and the word coupé – once used for two-seaters with a folding hood that was normally kept erected – now means any sporting saloon that is lower than average!

The pane of glass ahead of the folding rear roof section of this Fiat Tipo 4 (1) of c.1914 vintage identifies it as a three-quarter landaulette; a landaulette has the rear roof folding from immediately behind the door pillar. A sedan (2) of the traditional pattern is mounted on this 1931 Chevrolet. Chrysler, however, created a new name when they applied wood to the metal panelling of their Town and Country range: this 1949 two-seater (3) emphasizes the 'sporty-formal' ethos of that model. Designed to eliminate body rattles, the Weymann saloon (4), here mounted on a Peugeot, had lightweight wood framing with a leathercloth covering.

8

Two-seaters of a semi-sporting nature, like this 1938 Citroën 7cv (**5**), are often known as roadsters. The 1975 Lotus Elite (**6**) and the wicker-bodied Bugatti (**7**) show how specialist manufacturers are free of the styling constraints imposed on mass-producers. John Tjaarda styled the 1937 Lincoln-Zephyr V12 (**8**), one of the pioneering aerodynamic cars.

1931 to 1945

PERHAPS THE MOST significant pointer to the changing status of the motor car can be gauged from the fact that, at the beginning of the 1920s, the majority of cars were open tourers; by 1931, saloon bodies were fitted to 90 per cent of the cars produced. A contemporary editorial sums up the more functional, utilitarian role of the typical 1930s motor car: 'Today there is no room for the cheap and shoddy, or for immature design. The day has passed when unmechanical contraptions can claim the serious attention of the public... manufacturers no longer expect the public to carry out the testing of new productions for them'.

However, the public was also calling for smaller engines, more suited to the economic climate of the times. To cope with the weight of saloon bodywork and all the popular accessories, these little engines had to be geared low. Consequently they revved high and hard, and their bores wore alarmingly. The days when durability was a feature taken for granted on all but the shoddiest of cars seemed long past.

The design of cars now began to change radically as well. The demand for more capacious bodywork on small chassis led to the engine being pushed forward over the front axle. The radiator became a functional unit concealed behind a decorative grille which became more elaborate and exaggerated as the decade wore on until on some cars it resembled a chromium-plated waterfall or fencer's mask.

During the 1930–35 period, there was a vogue for streamlining which found its full flower in devices like the Chrysler Airflow, the Singer Airstream and the Fitzmaurice-bodied Ford V-8. Even on more staid cars, the angularity of line that had characterized the models of the late 1920s gave way to more flowing contours. Though most cars still retained running boards, the separate side valances were eliminated by bringing the lower door edges down to give a lower, more bulbous look, accentuated by the adoption of wings with side panels, often blended into the radiator and bonnet.

The swept tails of the new-style coachwork now usually concealed some kind of luggage accommodation as well, a feature sadly lacking on most 1920s models, which usually boasted a luggage grid and nothing more.

'Well-rounded and commodious', the cars of the 1930s offered greater comfort and convenience than their forebears. The stylist, however, had taken over from the engineer and the craftsman bodybuilder and, as a result, the new cars were often deficient in handling as the main masses were now concentrated at either end, like a dumb-bell. New suspension systems—especially independent front springing—also brought their handling problems, and some cars had to be fitted with bumpers incorporating a harmonic damping device to prevent them from

Henry Ford's 'last mechanical triumph' was his 1932 V8, seen here with phaeton bodywork.

shimmying right off the road on their supersoft springing.

Not that all was gloom and despondency in the 1930s: some manufacturers produced excellent cars during the decade. Morris and Austin continued to build soundly engineered small cars (though Herbert Austin was distinctly upset when his designers insisted on moving the radiator behind a dummy grille, as he felt that it was a kind of heresy), while the last two new models in which Henry Ford was personally involved, the 8hp Model 19Y and the V-8 (both appeared in 1932), were instantly and deservedly successful.

And, of course, there was the famous front-wheel-drive Citroën, which made its debut in 1934. Though its development costs had all but bankrupted André Citroën—who was forced to sell out to Michelin—this was one of the truly great cars.

A lesser, though no less significant, happening was the metamorphosis of the SS marque from a merely meretricious styling exercise into a modestly priced, excellently finished, well-equipped saloon—the first Jaguar.

The same year that the SS Jaguar was launched—1936—Dr Porsche built the prototype Volkswagens, the 'Strength through Joy' cars sponsored by the Nazi Party and intended to be sold to the German public at £50–£55 to keep them from buying imported models—the first of over 20 million of this most popular car of all time. Few Volkswagens, however, were built before the war (though the design was readily adapted for military purposes).

In many ways the 1930s were a watershed—they saw the last of the big luxury cars from makers such as Hispano-Suiza, Duesenberg and Minerva, as well as the end of many small, independent manufacturers and coachbuilders (victims of the swing to mass-produced cars with pressed-steel bodies). The motor industry had reached the point where it had become vital to the economic well-being of the major industrialized countries. Now it was to prove just as vital in providing weapons of war.

In Britain, five of the largest motor manufacturers set up 'shadow factories' in the late 1930s which could be used to produce aero engine parts in the event of war—they were to produce many thousands of aero engines and complete aircraft during the hostilities. Ford joined the five soon after the outbreak of war and was soon building Rolls-Royce Merlin engines on a moving production line in Manchester, while in the USA Ford mass-production expertise was given its greatest test in manufacturing Liberator bombers on a gigantic production line at Willow Run, Michigan.

From the ubiquitous Jeep, through staff cars, trucks, tanks and powerboats to the biggest bomber aircraft, the motor industry played a crucial role in World War Two. Re-adapting to peacetime production was, however, to prove almost as big a test of the industry's abilities.

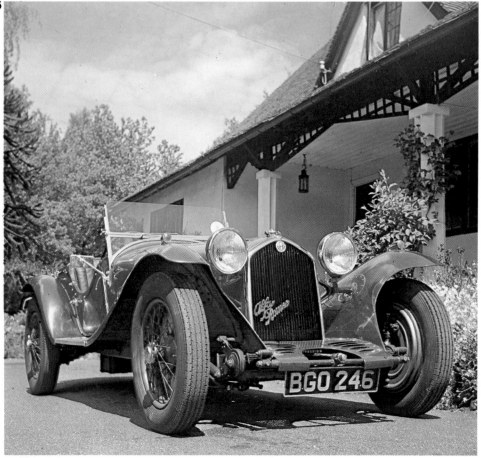

The 1930s saw a rapid evolution in body design, from traditional shapes like the Zagato-bodied 2.3-litre Alfa Romeo (**6**) – which nevertheless influenced the styling of many lesser breeds of sports car – to the avant-garde Cord (**1**) designed by Ray Dietrich and deemed worthy to be shown in New York's Museum of Modern Art. The Type 57 Bugatti (**2**) has saloon coachwork far more restrained than some of Jean Bugatti's creations on this chassis, while patrician marques like Packard (**3**) and Rolls-Royce (**4**) made some concessions to fashion while retaining their innate dignity. So, too, at a more humble level, did the Austin Seven (**5**).

Engines

Sophisticated and powerful though the engine of a modern car may be, nevertheless it operates on principles first successfully applied over a century ago. The first car engines were simple affairs, usually with one or two cylinders, though since the turn of the century multi-cylinder power units have predominated, normally with four, six or eight cylinders, though non-conformist configurations with three, five, twelve or sixteen cylinders have been tried. Rotary engines have also made sporadic appearances, too. But the main changes in the power unit have been technical improvements: the replacement of the atmospherically operated automatic inlet valve by mechanical inlet valves in the early 1900s, the adoption of monobloc cylinder castings instead of cylinders cast singly or in pairs, the general use of detachable cylinder heads, and the change from side to overhead valves. Today, the overhead camshaft, once the premise of high-powered sports and racing cars, is a common feature of family cars, thanks to the invention of the cogged driving belt, which replaces the complex gear trains of earlier designs and is cheap to install and silent in operation.

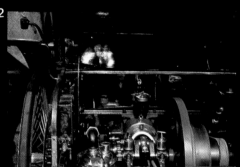

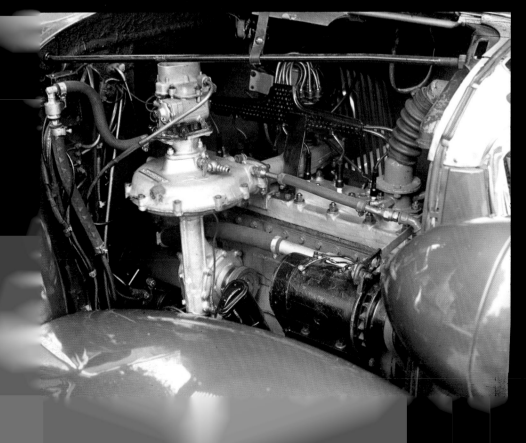

Engines developed rapidly: compare the 1908 Hutton (**1**) with its electrolytically-deposited copper water-jackets and dual ignition (the twin carburettors are an anachronism) with the primitive 1900 Benz (**2**) which has an exposed, grease-lubricated crankshaft like its 1885 forebear. The Jaguar XK120 engine, with its twin ohc (**3**) was a classic 1940s design capable of great development, while the 1934 Graham straight-eight, with its centrifugal supercharger (**4**), was a more short-lived way of obtaining increased performance.

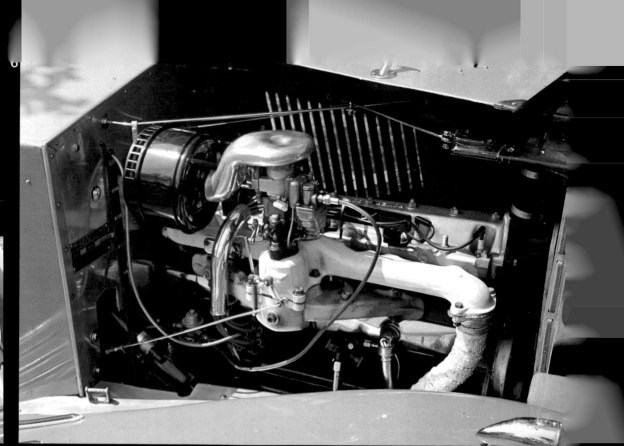

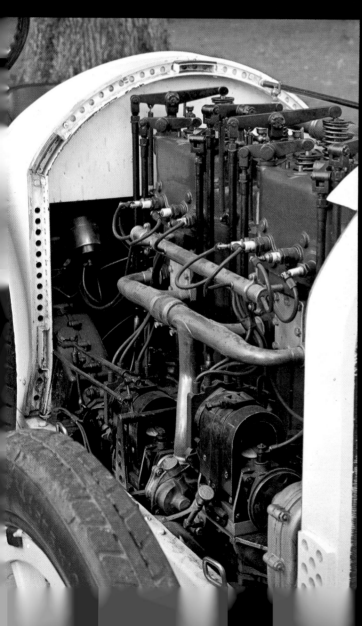

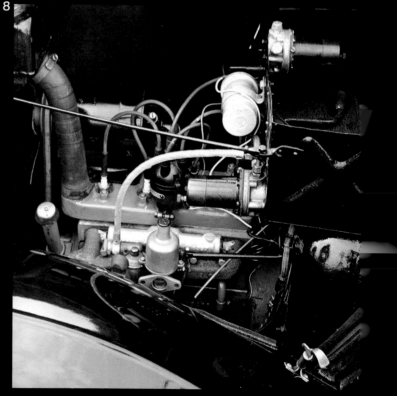

8

9

A more modestly priced dohc power unit was the Lotus Twin Cam, here seen in a 1971 Lotus Super Seven (**5**), while the Oldsmobile six in this 1936 Railton (**6**) was a simple side-valve unit relying on good power/weight ratio for performance. In more Wagnerian vein is the 1908 Grand Prix Benz unit (**7**), which promised plenty of *sturm und drang* with pushrod ohv and drainpipe exhaust. Measure it against the tiny sv engine of the 1936 Morris Eight (**8**) and the powerful American Ford V-8 of the 1970 AC Cobra (**9**).

1946 to 1960

BESET BY POST-WAR materials shortages and government interference, motor manufacturers nevertheless soon returned to production, inevitably with slightly modernized pre-war models in most cases though some manufacturers did actually manage to produce all-new cars, notably Armstrong-Siddeley in Britain.

Despite shortages of fuel and tyres, there was a vast demand in Britain for cars, but the government forced manufacturers to export half their output, even though these cars had been designed mostly for the very insular requirements of pre-war Britain. To curb the speculators who had been buying new cars and selling them at an inflated profit, purchasers had to sign a 'covenant' guaranteeing that they would not resell for initially one year, later two.

There was much talk of technical developments arising from wartime projects, but devices such as automatic transmission were only generally adopted in America, and reports that hydraulic suspension, or springing by rubber or torsion bars, were about to be adopted on British cars proved to be more than a little premature. Indeed, some makers seemed unready to come to terms with the future, as one report noted: 'Since wind resistance is an important factor in brake performance, streamlining may lead to braking difficulties, as was shown in experiments carried out in France'.

European manufacturers had also the problem of rebuilding war-shattered plant; in France, the industry had lost machine tools, equipment and labour to Germany and suffered much bomb damage. A shortage of sheet steel and tyres also helped to keep production to about a sixth of the 1938 level in 1946–48, though some recovery was apparent by 1949 when the first post-war Salon de l'Automobile was held in Paris and production had risen to about four times the 1938 monthly level.

Other manufacturing countries had similar difficulties, those of Germany being compounded by the division of the country and the replacement of the Reichsmark (£1 = RM24) by the Deutschmark (£1 = DM11.75), an effective devaluation of around 100 per cent. Nevertheless, the country's most prolific manufacturer, Volkswagen, continued to make progress despite opinions from British experts—and from Henry Ford II—that the VW was too noisy and uncomfortable to be competitive. And though the BMW factory had ended up in the Russian Zone, the first—and only—'war reparation' design to come out of Germany became the BMW-based Bristol 400.

That was only one of the classic sports cars to appear after the war; more famous still was the Jaguar XK 120, with a twin-cam engine reportedly developed during wartime firewatching duty. It made its debut in 1948 along with two, more utilitarian, designs — the Morris Minor and the Citroën 2 cv.

A classic post-war sports car, the Jaguar XK 120

Built by the most traditionally minded motor company of all, the Morgan 4/4 (**1**) of the 1950s was little changed in appearance from its ancestor of the mid-1930s. Like all Morgans built since 1910, it had sliding-pillar independent front suspension. The advanced and complex Citroën DS (**2**) supplanted the immortal *traction avant* in 1955. The 1946 Lincoln (**3**) shows how even quality post-war American cars adopted extreme styling for their radiator grilles.

The 1950s saw the motor industry entering a period of traumatic change. Those brave attempts by independent companies like Kaiser and Crosley to carve a foothold in the American market against the corporate giants of the Big Three—Ford, GM and Chrysler—came to nothing, and the most respected of the old-established independents like Packard, Nash and Studebaker were in decline and would soon vanish, either by attrition or by merger. The American car industry had become stereotyped. Its typical product—generally superlatively hideous—had either a six-cylinder engine (often of fairly antique provenance) or a V-8, and boasted excruciatingly named accessories and components like Hi-Fyre or Firedome engines, HydraMatic or UltraMatic transmissions, even FlightSweep styling. This was the era of the exaggerated tailfin and the grinning chrome grille, and the 'performance car' that could only go fast in a straight line. The announcement of small 'compact' cars in 1959 brought, as well as the Ford Falcon and Chrysler Valiant of conventional design, the unorthodox rear-engined Chevrolet Corvair whose unAmerican handling activities ensured that the US industry went straight from nadir to Nader.

There were mergers in Europe, too, like the shotgun wedding between Austin and Morris, a union born out of strife which would lay the seeds of trouble for that British Motor Corporation's ultimate descendant, British Leyland. But, at that time, their products—small family cars—were just what the public wanted. Fuel economy became even more significant after the 1956 Suez War, when petrol was rationed, and the event created a new race of cyclecars, only now they called them 'bubblecars', and many of them came from German firms grounded in the aircraft industry like Heinkel and Messerschmitt.

In the main, these bubblecars were beastly machines whose only merit lay in their economy; their death-knell was tolled by the advent of an epochal design by Alec Issigonis—the 1959 Mini Minor, which gave a new word to the popular vocabulary and heralded a new race of decently engineered small cars with sports car-like handling. Its layout of front-wheel drive and transverse engine was to set the pattern for the coming 20 years and more.

But the 1950s had their glamour cars, too: Britain produced the big Healeys, the Triumph TRs and the first MG to abandon the perperpendicular lines of the 1930s, the slippery profiled MGA, even available with a temperamental twin-cam engine; Italy built big, powerful sports cars like the Ferrari America and Super America; France, which had taxed the *grand'routiers* like Delahaye out of existence, introduced the avant-garde Citroën DS; and Germany, once again *persona grata* after its post-war isolation, brought out the unique and distinctive Mercedes 300SL coupé, with its stylish, if not entirely practical, gull-wing doors.

One of the most sought-after sports cars of the 1950s, both then and now, was the 300SL Mercedes (**4**), with its unorthodox gull-wing doors. Cadillac set the fashion for fins in the 1950s: by the 1954 models (**5**) this vulgar trend had reached its peak.

5

Dashboards

Though the very first cars were devoid of instruments, by 1899 enterprising accessory manufacturers had begun to offer speedometers: 'motor timepieces' soon followed, along with voltmeters, gradient meters, odometers and petrol gauges. The first 'idiot lights' appeared in 1908 in the shape of a patent oil indicating device which glowed white when there was sufficient oil, red when the level was too low. The invention of the dipstick soon rendered this 'Lubrimeter' superfluous. By 1910, there was even an instrument to measure petrol consumption. Some of these ingenious devices, too far ahead of their time to be commercially viable, have been 're-invented' and, in modern form, appear on some of the latest cars.

Compare the traditional approach of the instrument panel on the 1959 R-type Continental Bentley (**1**) with the modern approach (**2**) of the 1979 Saab 900 saloon, with padded steering wheel for safety. The 1951 Porsche 356 Speedster's instrument panel (**3**) reflects the character both of the car and of the era in which it was built.

3

The complex instrumentation of the 1929 Mercedes 38/250 SS (**4**) is appropriate to a high-performance supercharged car, yet its racing ancestor, the 1908 Benz (**5**) has a bare minimum of instruments, most importantly the drip indicator which shows that oil is going to the engine bearings in sufficient quantity. The 1979 Panther J72 (**6**) represents an attempt to blend traditional dash layout with modern safety requirements. In late-1920s American cars, like the 1929 Stutz Blackhawk (**7**), the hand of the stylist appeared to be set against easy interpretation of the instrument readings, a defect shared by the 1958 Chevrolet dash (**8**). The 1979 Aston Martin (**9**), however, represents a return to classicism (though its stablemate, the Lagonda, made extensive use of digital readouts).

1961 to 1979

THE VERY SUCCESS of the American compact cars brought new problems to their makers in the early 1960s. For, instead of capturing a whole new market, they encroached into established sales areas, and American dealers began the decade with upwards of a million unsold 'full-size' cars on their hands. Not only that, but the compacts also hit exports of European cars to the USA, and many dealers just stopped selling foreign cars. The only two makes which really managed to hang on to their American sales were Volkswagen and Renault; interestingly enough, in the late 1970s these two firms were to remain most heavily committed to the USA market, VW opening a plant in Pennsylvania in 1978 which gave them third place in sales in a remarkably short space of time, and Renault tying up a sales deal with AMC (which VW had pushed into fourth place).

America was making its presence felt in Europe, too. Ford of America took control of its English affiliate for a record sum of money, and Chrysler began a step-by-step takeover of the Rootes Group with governmental blessing, the task of sorting out the company's financial problems having been judged beyond the powers of mere government officials.

Mergers were the order of the day, for Standard-Triumph joined up with the Leyland Group in 1960, and the same year Jaguar and Daimler combined. Jaguar-Daimler was itself absorbed by the BMC in 1966, while Leyland took over Rover (which had acquired Alvis). Finally, Leyland and the BMC merged early in 1967, after much hard bargaining (though as a prime reason for the merger had been political rather than commercial, the huge and complex group faced extraordinary difficulties right from the start). The result was British Leyland, which later became BL. The problems it inherited included model lines which competed with one another, thus reducing group efficiency, and the fact that their most outstanding popular model, the Mini, was being produced at a loss—indeed, it was to reach its twentieth birthday before it showed a profit.

German manufacturers were uniting, too: Mercedes had already linked with Auto-Union-DKW, and Volkswagen and NSU also became part of the same grouping during the decade, while the old two-stroke DKW was succeeded by a revived Audi marque. In France, Citroën took over Panhard, one of the industry's oldest marques, in 1965, but ended car production there two years later.

There were many reasons why Europe's manufacturers were joining together—as well as direct mergers, the decade also saw the start of programmes of cooperation jointly to develop components such as engines for the benefit of several makers, who perhaps could

Named after Enzo Ferrari's dead son, the Dino brought Ferrari-style motoring to a wider circle. This is a 1972 model.

not stand the ever-increasing cost of developing new power plants on their own.

And there was a new source of competition as well, for the Japanese were beginning to send their cars to Europe in small numbers. It was the start of an onslaught which was to become such a torrent that, in little over a decade, manufacturers from some European countries—especially Britain—had to strike a 'gentleman's agreement' with the Japanese manufacturers that the latter would hold down exports to a 'prudent' level, since it was felt that their products were placing too much stress on the indigenous manufacturers. Just how good the Japanese products had become was to be emphasized in 1979, when BL announced that it was to build a Honda model as a stopgap.

A crucial turning point in the history of the automobile came with the Arab embargo on oil exports following the Arab-Israeli War of late 1973. Though supplies were gradually restored to something approaching normality, the system had suffered a shock from which it would perhaps never fully recover, for the era of cheap oil was over.

For America, the experience was particularly traumatic, for the public had become accustomed to unlimited use of big, 'gas-guzzling' cars. Shortages in petrol supply gave Americans a chilling reminder of what life without cars could mean. The eventual result, once panic measures like the virtually overnight switching of production from large models to compacts had subsided, was an almost nationwide blanket speed limit of 55 mph and government insistence on the production of more fuel-efficient cars for the 1980s. There was even, following post-revolutionary cuts in petrol supplies from Iran, the introduction in 1979 of rationing in California, where three-car families were common. This represented a dramatic turnabout in future model policies, and involved vast expenditure. For Ford in 1978, the outlay needed to develop new, more economical cars for the early 1980s fuel consumption limits was greater than the total sum of investment over the company's previous 75 years. For General Motors, it represented an annual bill of $3·2 billion from 1975 on to revise its model range, an increase of 135 per cent on previous years. And for Chrysler, finance had to be found by selling off most of its foreign holdings, notably Chrysler Europe, acquired by Peugeot-Citroën.

In fact, Europe was now the focus of the world car industry. The European manufacturers had overtaken the output of American firms in the late 1960s, and, by the end of the 1970s, were building about 20 per cent more. Long conditioned by higher petrol prices and fiscal restrictions on engine size, Europe had developed smaller, more efficient cars.

In less than a century, the motor car has totally changed society, and become vital to the economic life of many nations. But what does the next century hold for the motor car?

2

3

4

6

A group of cars which epitomizes the face of motoring in the 1970s. The 1978 Chrysler (now Talbot) Sunbeam (**1**) is typical of the modern breed of small hatchback cars. Porsche's 928 (**2**) is one of the ultimate sporting cars, while the Range Rover (**3**), with its go-anywhere four-wheel drive, is a practical workhorse as well as a status symbol leisure vehicle. Oldsmobile's Omega (**4**) is one of their 1980 'X-cars', designed to incorporate more 'European' characteristics than earlier American models. Aston Martin's 1979 V8 (**5**) and the Bertone-styled Fiat X1/9 (**6**) show opposite ends of the sporting scale.

Art and the automobile

Since automobile art first arose in Paris at the turn of the century, mainly taking the form of caricatures and allegorical posters, it has embraced many forms and schools of art, being particularly evident in the contemporary Pop Art and Photo Realism movements in the USA. Popular items for collectors of 'automobiliana' include posters, sculptures, mascots, ornaments, glassware, even 'polychrome sculptural masses' formed from car components fed into a hydraulic press.

3

An 1898 poster (1) by Belgian racing cyclist Georges Gaudy, this was one of the first posters to advertise a motor race; the car is probably a Benz, and the driver, Old Father Time. More serious artists are painting car subjects today than at any time in the past, and nowhere is this more evident than in the Pop Art and Photo Realism movements; this example of the Photo Realism school is *Wrecking Yard III* (2) by the American Don Eddy. (3) A squared-up drawing and water-colour by Geo Ham (Georges Hamel), a famous French illustrator most active in the 1930s and 1940s.

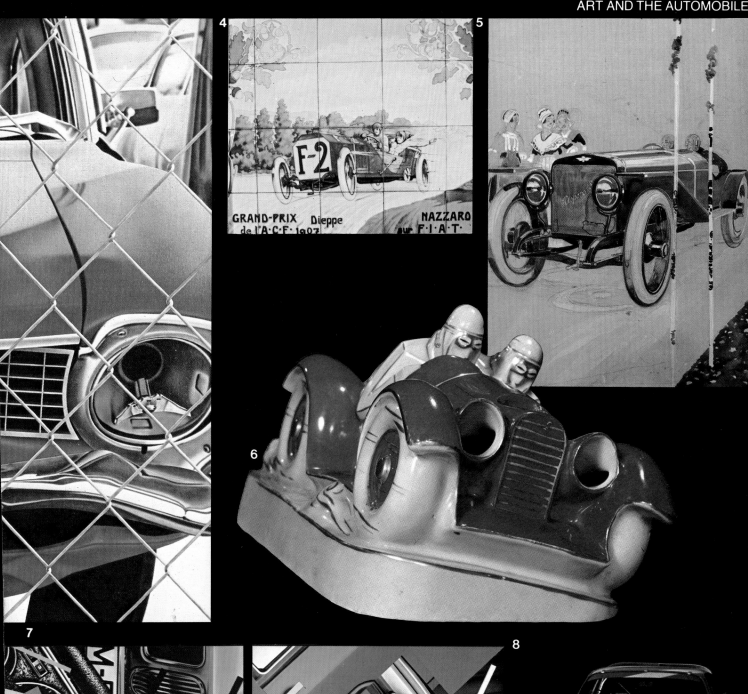

4

GRAND-PRIX Dieppe
de l'A·C·F·1907
NAZZARO
sur F·I·A·T·

5

6

7

8

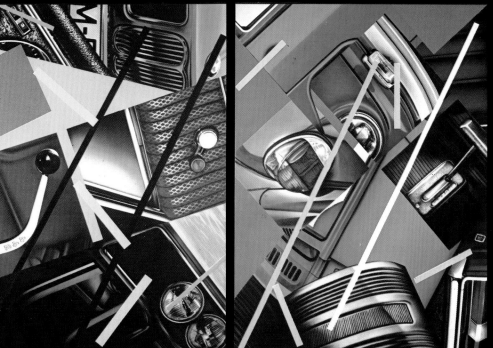

The Michelin Tyre Company's building in Fulham
Road, London, was the work of architect François
Espinasse. Dating from 1910, it is decorated with
coloured tiles depicting contemporary racing
successes; this scene (4) is of the 1907 French
Grand Prix. The Hispano-Suiza catalogue (5) was
illustrated by René Vincent, a leading motoring
artist from before World War One to the 1930s.
(6) Motoring ornaments are widely collected items
of 'automobiliana'; this is a porcelain Art Deco
example. Automobilia (7) is a 1960s Pop Art
composition by Peter Philips. (8) A 3.5-litre BMW
decorated by American sculptor Alexander
Calder, inventor of the 'mobile'.

The evolution of mass production

THE PHENOMENAL GROWTH of the car industry would not have been possible without the introduction of mass-production methods. It is generally thought that mass production was invented by Henry Ford, and introduced in his Highland Park, Detroit, factory in 1913. Yet Ford was only applying the lessons of over 100 years' progress in large-scale manufacturing.

As far back as 1798, Eli Whitney, given a rush order for 10,000 muskets by the United States Government, built machines that duplicated gun parts so accurately that they could quickly be assembled into finished muskets without hand fitting. He demonstrated this by scrambling the parts of 10 muskets and then assembling a musket from parts taken at random.

Contemporaneously, Marc Brunel (father of Isambard Kingdom Brunel) was supplying the British Navy with rigging blocks produced on automatic machines at Portsmouth Dockyard—'machinery so perfect appears to act with the happy certainty of instinct, and the foresight of reason combined', wrote one visitor. The machines were produced in association with Henry Maudslay, whose standardization of screw threads and accurate lathes and planing machinery brought the standards of precision that would make mass production truly feasible.

Another vital feature of mass production, the moving conveyor belt, had appeared in 1783 in an automatic grain mill devised by Oliver Evans, who later built one of America's first

Today, mass-production car factories are making increasing use of computers to control production processes, as in the Fiat works (**below**). However, there has also been a revival in 'traditional' hand production methods for limited-production cars, as in the Panther factory (**bottom and below right**).

steam carriages. Evans's mill used belt, bucket and screw conveyors, and could be operated by only two men, one pouring grain into a hopper at one end of the mill, the other putting flour into sacks at the other end.

The technique was carried a stage further in the Chicago meat factories from the 1860s, when the meat packers adopted the method of hanging pigs from an overhead conveyor, so that all the operations from slaughtering to jointing were carried out by a series of workers, each carrying out a single operation on the carcass. It took just four minutes from catching a pig in the stock pen until its carcass arrived in the cooling room to be turned into hams, sausages and pork chops. Output was more than doubled.

The idea that output could be multiplied by dividing work had been given impetus by Elihu Root, who joined Samuel Colt's armament factory in 1849 and boosted production of Colt Six Shooters by dividing and simplifying the steps in their manufacture and inventing new machinery to fill the gaps in the sequence.

Frederick Winslow Taylor, a contemporary of Henry Ford, was the original 'efficiency expert', who devised time and motion studies based on the theory that production was fastest when worker efficiency was highest.

Such ideas were more likely to find a receptive audience in America, where skilled labour was scarce and expensive, and American metalworking machinery had become the best in the world by the dawn of the motor age. The Lanchester brothers in Britain were thought remarkable for insisting on rigorous interchangeability of parts; in America, interchangeability was a necessity, though men like Henry Leland, schooled in the high standards of

the arms industry, did bring it to a high pitch.

But all the early American mass-production motor manufacturers worked in similar ways: chassis were erected where they stood, parts being brought to them. It worked well enough in industries like the manufacture of sewing machines or typewriters (where America also excelled) but was clumsy where cars were being made in great numbers.

Progress towards more effective production was rapid. White, for example, had an overhead craneway running the full 600ft length of their Cleveland plant, feeding the buildings branching off on either side (though a similar scheme had been used by J. G. Bodmer in England in 1839). Chalmers-Detroit had a chassis assembly room by 1909 in which frames were ranged in two parallel rows, with overhead tracks bringing in motors and other heavy parts at the appropriate moment.

But mass production as we know it today resulted from Henry Ford's combining all the best features of these pioneering ventures in his newly completed Highland Park plant in Detroit in 1913. Ford constantly experimented with gravity slides, conveyors, and the placement of men and tools for maximum efficiency. Breaking each manufacturing operation into its constituent parts, he multiplied the production of anything from flywheel magnetos to complete engines, often by a factor of four.

Department by department he established sub-assembly lines until, in his own words, 'everything in the plant moved'.

The ultimate step was the creation of the moving final assembly line, where the chassis itself moved, starting without wheels at one end of the line and emerging at the other end as a completed car, driven off under its own power.

One of the first Ford components to be mass produced was the flywheel magneto (**right**). This remarkable series of photographs was taken in the Ford Highland Park plant in 1915 to illustrate the first-ever book on mass-production of motor vehicles. Carefully synchronized feeder lines supplied components to the final assembly line, and the mass-production thus made possible enabled prices to be cut and, simultaneously, the minimum daily wage at Ford to be raised to $5. Model Ts came forth in ever-increasing numbers at ever-decreasing prices until a car was leaving the production lines every 10 seconds, at prices as low as $260 (around £50), and an annual production figure of 2,000,000 was achieved.

How cars are made

THE BUILDING OF A CAR begins with the manufacture of its individual components—up to 15,000 of them. Some of the steel components are forged or cast, but most are made from sheet steel pressed into hundreds of different shapes by huge presses capable of exerting pressures of up to 2000 tons per square inch.

The pressings are carried by fork-lift trucks to the pre-production line workshops, and in separate processes the building of the superstructure and underbody begins. First, small sub-assemblies are put together by spot welding. Then these are fitted into jigs, which hold the pieces in place as they are joined by automatic welders; from these the major superstructure and underbody emerge complete. Modern body

weld units can complete up to 1000 welds simultaneously with absolute accuracy.

Now the doors, plus bonnet and boot lid—all arriving ready-made by overhead monorail conveyor—are fitted. Major panel joints have been gas-welded to give greater strength and flexibility when the car is under stress from cornering or rough roads. Finally the bodywork is prepared for painting; each body shell will be finished in plain or metallic colours to an individual order tapped out by teleprinter.

The car is degreased by high-pressure sprays and phosphated to provide a good anti-corrosion and paint adhesion surface; the body is then stoved. Now the car is totally immersed in an electrocoat primer paint process. This

provides a paint film on all areas of the body, including those box sections which are inaccessible under normal processes. The surplus paint is rinsed off and the body is stoved in a gas-fired oven. All outer joints are sealed before the body passes through electrostatic paint spraying equipment. This automatically applies a grey primer sealing coat, which is then stoved. A protective material is applied to the underbody. Each body is wet sanded, rinsed with de-mineralized water and finally dried. The car is then ready to receive three top coats of enamel paint which is applied manually and stoved in a steam-heated oven.

The cars now move on to the trim shop; each has already acquired an individual identity, and

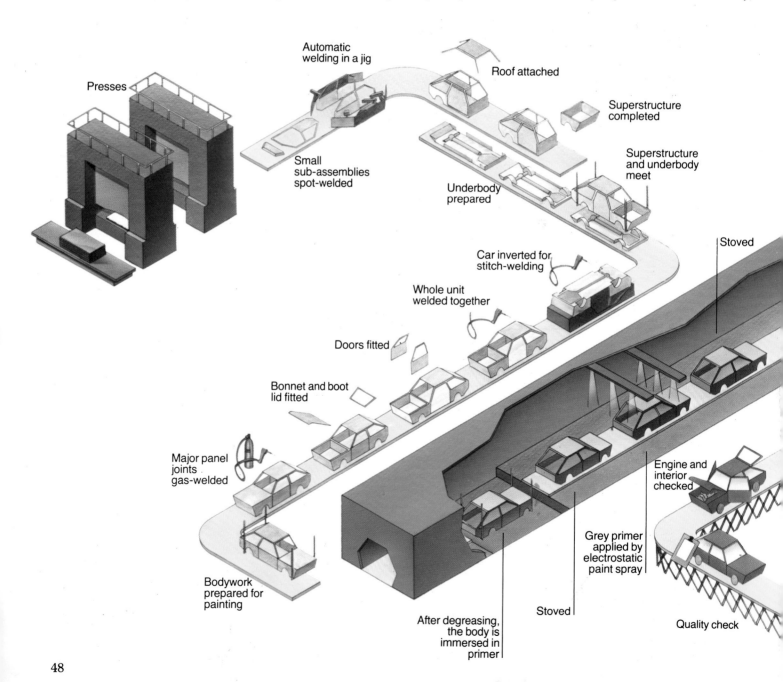

Presses

Automatic welding in a jig

Roof attached

Superstructure completed

Small sub-assemblies spot-welded

Underbody prepared

Superstructure and underbody meet

Stoved

Car inverted for stitch-welding

Whole unit welded together

Doors fitted

Bonnet and boot lid fitted

Major panel joints gas-welded

Engine and interior checked

Grey primer applied by electrostatic paint spray

Bodywork prepared for painting

Stoved

After degreasing, the body is immersed in primer

Quality check

details of its trim specification are transferred from a teleprinter to a card on the bonnet. The build-up starts as components stockpiled beside the production line are fitted—the grille, electrical wiring, lights, head lining, door windows, windscreen.

Then come the under-bonnet parts like horns, battery, brake fluid reservoirs, steering column, radiator and pipes, as well as the instrument panel. Nowadays, much of the complex wiring loom has been eliminated by printed circuits and plug-in modules.

The engine, having been given a 'hot' running test, arrives at the production line complete with carburettors, exhaust manifold, alternator and fan. The clutch/gearbox unit, drive shaft, rear axle, front and rear suspensions—including hubs and brakes—are fitted in a special jig and everything is bolted together. The engine/transmission/suspension assembly moves forward to meet the line from the body shops; the correct body unit is lowered to meet it. The nearly completed car now moves along a raised line. The wipers and interior trim are fitted; the radiator is filled and hydraulic fluid fed into the brake system.

Wheels, made in a separate plant and already fitted with tyres, arrive on a gravity conveyor and are bolted on, and the car rolls forward on its own for the first time. Fuel is added to the tank.

Seats are the last item to be added to the interior. The engine idles as it is checked; then suspension and steering settings are adjusted and checked.

After a final examination of the trim the car undergoes a quality check before it goes on to the roller testing station to test the engine, transmission, steering, brakes and lights. A diagnostic unit checks that the electrical circuit is fully functional. The car is driven on to a conveyorized water test where jets of water at 20 psi are directed on to the cars for four minutes as they pass through the tunnel.

Dried down, it has its final check, then it is parked in the trade compound to await the dealer's delivery conveyor lorries to take it to the showroom.

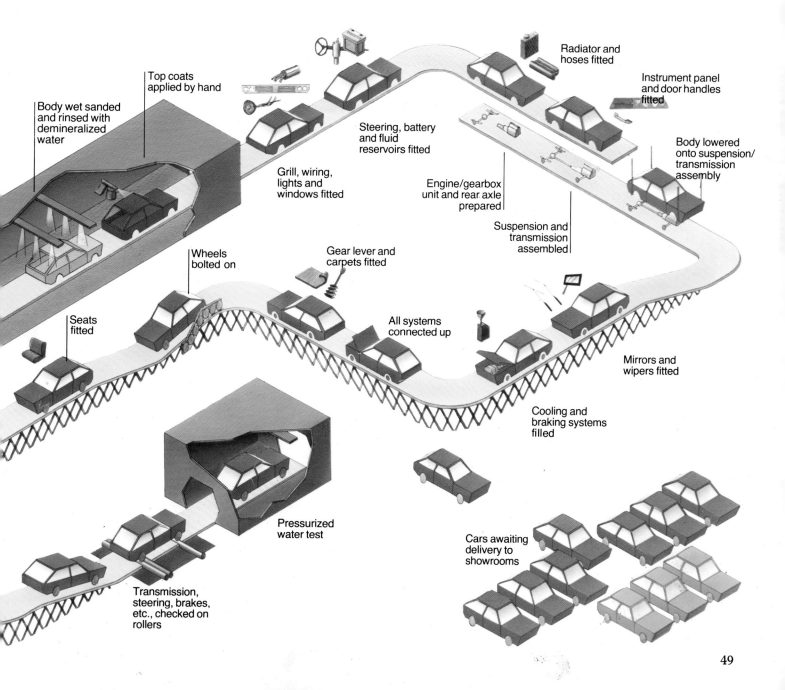

Body wet sanded and rinsed with demineralized water

Top coats applied by hand

Radiator and hoses fitted

Instrument panel and door handles fitted

Steering, battery and fluid reservoirs fitted

Grill, wiring, lights and windows fitted

Engine/gearbox unit and rear axle prepared

Body lowered onto suspension/ transmission assembly

Suspension and transmission assembled

Wheels bolted on

Gear lever and carpets fitted

Seats fitted

All systems connected up

Mirrors and wipers fitted

Cooling and braking systems filled

Pressurized water test

Cars awaiting delivery to showrooms

Transmission, steering, brakes, etc., checked on rollers

Developing a new car

A NEW CAR USUALLY starts as a designer's concept, based on a number of assumptions, known as the 'package', which specify the broad outlines of the vehicle—how many passengers the vehicle must accommodate, the layout of engine, transmission and suspension, and the luggage space. Length, width, height, wheelbase and passenger compartment dimensions are also laid down—the cost of developing a new car these days is so great that it must be designed to fill a perceived gap in the market or to succeed a well-established success. Cars are no longer launched in the fond belief that merit alone will sell them.

Each new programme results in a number of sketches for further development, and the best of these are developed into more detailed illustrations—'renderings'—to evaluate the design's potential.

A wheeled 'armature'—a wood and foam plastic skeleton slightly smaller than the finished vehicle—is covered in a special modelling clay, applied warm and shaped to the contours of the design rendering by highly skilled clay modellers. Frequently referring to full-scale brush renderings or fullsize line drawings, the modellers scrape and form the clay using a wide variety of special tools, many of their own manufacture. Because the clay is so malleable, it can be reshaped easily until the designer is satisfied with the appearance of the model.

Now the clay can be 'finished' to give it a realistic appearance. A glossy skin of thin plastic sheet can be applied to simulate paintwork, a similar material gives the impression of windows, and metal foil represents the brightwork.

If the finished clay is approved, a glass-fibre moulding can be taken. This can be fitted with seats, trim and instrument panel (which have already been developed by a separate design team) to give a very good idea of the final form the car will take. Usually, a number of models is made for assessment.

These days, the techniques of the market researcher are often called in to ensure that the production vehicle will appeal to the motoring public. Before one popular model was put into production, the various prototypes were assembled in secret in a hall in Switzerland, and potential buyers flown in from Britain, Germany, Italy, France and Spain to assess these designs and compare them with competitive vehicles. Similar 'clinics' were held in the USA, South America, Spain and Germany. Additionally, surveys questioned over 5000 members of the public on what they expected in terms of engine size, options, specifications and serviceability in such a vehicle. The answers, surprisingly uniform, showed that the designers were on the right track.

During the development stages, a design changes continually, especially now that the

A draughtsman makes a full-size drawing of a proposed new model so that critical dimensions can be evaluated (**left**). Because of the cost of building full-size prototypes, fifth-scale models of a new car are made so that wind-tunnel tests can be carried out to 'fine-tune' the aerodynamics before a project is committed to sheet metal (**above**). Using modelling clay, highly skilled modellers create not only full-size mockups of a new design, but also interior features like the facia panel (**right**).

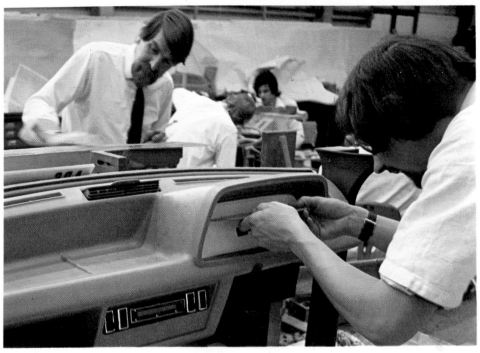

wind-tunnel is an indispensable part of the design equipment. One family car went through over 250 detail body changes as a result of wind-tunnel testing.

Wind-tunnel testing has produced such features of modern car design as front-end air dams and rear-end spoilers; it has contributed to more economical engines and improved roadholding at speed.

Computers are playing an increased role in car body development, too: the principle is to analyze half of the complete body, which, as the vehicle is virtually symmetrical about a longitudinal centre line, gives information for the whole car.

The input of loads on a vehicle can be computer-simulated, and the computer then calulates the resultant stress distribution throughout the structure. Individual panels can be studied under tension and compression, torsion and bending. Redundant members can be eliminated and panel strengths maximized while still reducing overall weight.

The computer can go beyond designing the basic structure and showing how it will perform in normal service: it can also run crash tests on the theoretical structure. By simulating barrier crash tests on a 'hybrid-analogue' computer, effective 'management' of the energy absorbed in a crash can be arranged. One computer-designed body shell was given an actual crash test when it was found it performed exactly as

Crash behaviour of new models is assessed in controlled tests (**above**), though today much of the information that used to be gained by destroying expensive prototypes can be gained from computer programmes. Unwanted noises can be detected and eliminated by running tests in an anechoic chamber (**left**), a totally soundless environment. Wind-tunnel tests on the completed prototype (**right**) produce much valuable information.

forecast—the displacement of the steering column into the driving compartment was accurately predicted, and the doors still opened after the impact.

However, computer analysis is only part of the body design process, and must be verified by accelerated tests on the track and in the laboratory. Much valuable time can be saved by simulating the effect of rough roads on a test rig which feeds shock loads into a prototype metal body shell by means of hydraulic rams attached to the suspension pickup points. Tape recordings taken from a test car running across a proving track feed in 'real-life' torsion and bending loads. Finally, prototypes are given extended tests on the manufacturer's proving grounds, where all types of road surface are reproduced and where years of normal use can be condensed into a few weeks.

In fact, before any modern car is put on sale, every component will have been subjected to thousands of test cycles, prototypes will have been deliberately destroyed to prove the protection given by the passenger compartment in accidents, and cost of servicing and maintenance will have been exhaustively analyzed.

The manufacturer will have spent anything up to a billion dollars to develop this new model, and in the end its commercial success or failure still rely on whether the motorist finds it attractive and sound value for money. That is the most crucial test of all.

A global industry

TRADITIONALLY, CAR PRODUCTION has been mainly centred in the northern United States and north-western Europe, with Japan playing an increasingly important role since the 1950s. But now other countries are important car producers. For example, when production of VW's Beetle was phased out in Germany, this robust design continued to be built in Brazil and Nigeria, where its relative simplicity of design made it more suitable for local conditions than more modern and sophisticated designs. And the so-called 'Third World' countries, where labour costs are low, may soon move into world markets as inexorably as the Japanese have done. Already the first South Korean cars have reached Europe, establishing a 'beach-head' for imports from this Asian country whose motor industry is only a few years old (even though, as far back as 1912, it was claimed that the Koreans called all cars 'Ford' because there were so many Model Ts on their roads).

Conversely, the major European and American manufacturers are actively moving into new manufacturing markets, like Egypt, Morocco or Kenya, competing for market supremacy in Mexico, Argentina or Venezuela, and expanding into new European markets like Spain and Portugal.

In the case of the two American giants (Ford and GM), these overseas markets were vital to their continued success in the USA, where a slaving domestic market and the vast expense of meeting the Government's corporate average fuel economy (CAFE) limits meant that, to finance the cars of the 1980s, manufacturers needed the volume that only the world market could supply.

For the third-biggest US company, Chrysler, the cost of meeting CAFE and of developing new models for the 1980s prompted entrenchment and the selling-off of most of its overseas subsidiaries to raise revenue.

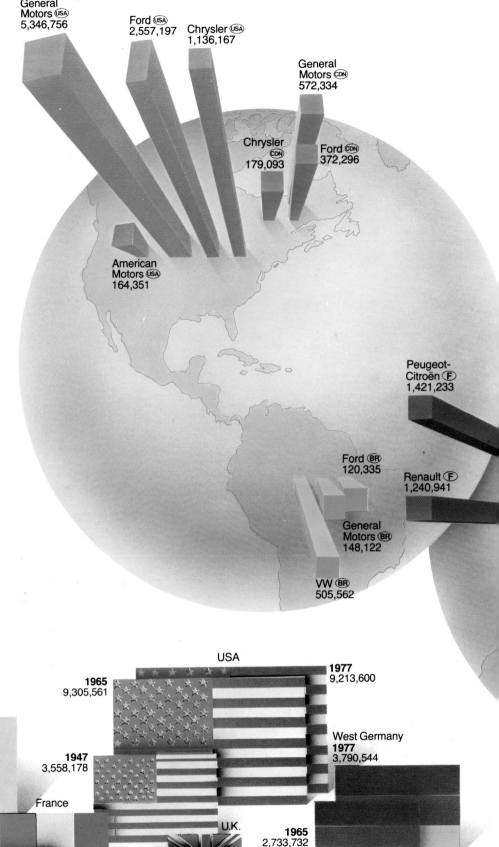

General Motors (USA) 5,346,756
Ford (USA) 2,557,197
Chrysler (USA) 1,136,167
General Motors (CDN) 572,334
Chrysler (CDN) 179,093
Ford (CDN) 372,296
American Motors (USA) 164,351
Peugeot-Citroën (F) 1,421,233
Ford (BR) 120,335
Renault (F) 1,240,941
General Motors (BR) 148,122
VW (BR) 505,562

Production figures for the principal car manufacturing countries for the years 1947, 1965 and 1977

USA
1965 9,305,561
1977 9,213,600
1947 3,558,178

Japan
1977 5,431,045
1965 696,176
1947 110

France
1977 3,092,439
1965 1,423,365
1947 66,277

West Germany
1977 3,790,544
1965 2,733,732

U.K.
1977 1,327,820
1965 1,722,045
1947 287,000

Sweden
1947 2,545
1965 181,755
1977 235,383

Canada
1977 1,161,314
1965 710,711
1947 167,257

Italy
1977 1,440,470
1947 23,375
1965 1,103,932
1947 9,541

54

The World's Leading Car Manufacturers (1978 figures)

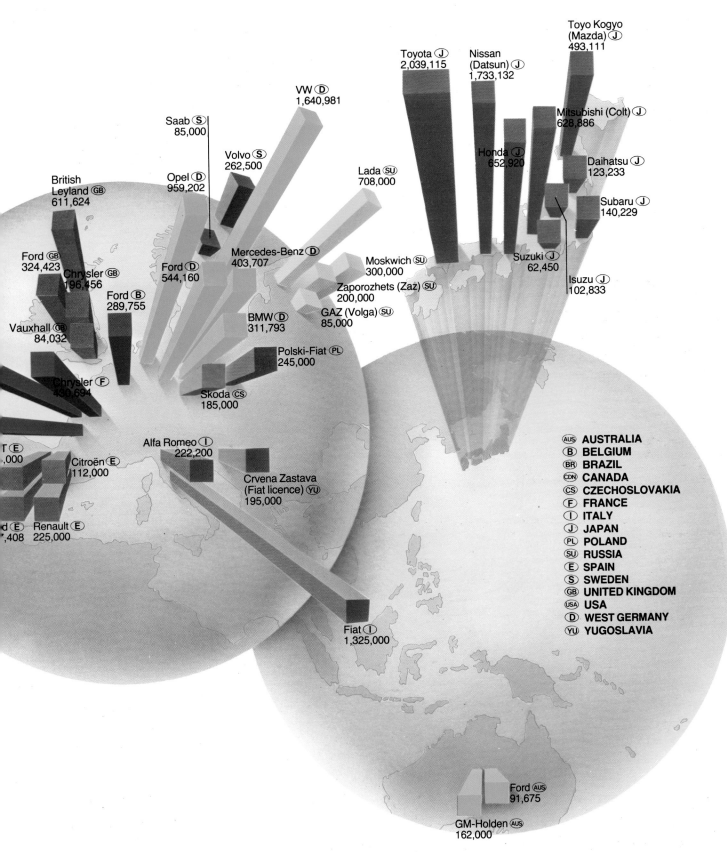

Toyo Kogyo (Mazda) Ⓙ
493,111

Toyota Ⓙ
2,039,115

Nissan (Datsun) Ⓙ
1,733,132

Mitsubishi (Colt) Ⓙ
628,886

Honda Ⓙ
652,920

Daihatsu Ⓙ
123,233

VW Ⓓ
1,640,981

Saab Ⓢ
85,000

Volvo Ⓢ
262,500

Opel Ⓓ
959,202

Lada ⓈⓊ
708,000

Subaru Ⓙ
140,229

British Leyland ⒼⒷ
611,624

Mercedes-Benz Ⓓ
403,707

Ford Ⓓ
544,160

Ford ⒼⒷ
324,423

Chrysler ⒼⒷ
196,456

Moskwich ⓈⓊ
300,000

Suzuki Ⓙ
62,450

Ford Ⓑ
289,755

Zaporozhets (Zaz) ⓈⓊ
200,000

Isuzu Ⓙ
102,833

Vauxhall ⒼⒷ
84,032

BMW Ⓓ
311,793

GAZ (Volga) ⓈⓊ
85,000

Chrysler Ⓕ
430,694

Polski-Fiat ⓅⓁ
245,000

Skoda ⒸⓈ
185,000

Ⓔ
,000

Citroën Ⓔ
112,000

Alfa Romeo Ⓘ
222,200

Crvena Zastava (Fiat licence) ⓎⓊ
195,000

d Ⓔ
,408

Renault Ⓔ
225,000

Fiat Ⓘ
1,325,000

Ford ⒶⓊⓈ
91,675

GM-Holden ⒶⓊⓈ
162,000

ⒶⓊⓈ **AUSTRALIA**
Ⓑ **BELGIUM**
Ⓑⓡ **BRAZIL**
Ⓒⓓⓝ **CANADA**
ⒸⓈ **CZECHOSLOVAKIA**
Ⓕ **FRANCE**
Ⓘ **ITALY**
Ⓙ **JAPAN**
ⓅⓁ **POLAND**
ⓈⓊ **RUSSIA**
Ⓔ **SPAIN**
Ⓢ **SWEDEN**
ⒼⒷ **UNITED KINGDOM**
ⓊⓈⒶ **USA**
Ⓓ **WEST GERMANY**
ⓎⓊ **YUGOSLAVIA**

Alternative power sources

THOUGH THE FOUR-STROKE internal combustion engine has been around for over a century, it has had remarkably few challengers to its supremacy.

In the early days of motoring, steam and electricity both had their advocates, but their shortcomings led to their general demise. Steam—external combustion—needed a boiler and water tank, and was complex to operate and maintain, while the electric car needed heavy accumulators to give even the most modest of ranges; it enjoyed something of a vogue in America as a town car, however, up to the 1920s.

Once the electric starter was a commonplace item of equipment, the supremacy of the petrol engine was assured, until, that is, fuel shortages inspired manufacturers to search for viable alternatives. During World War One, cars had been run on coal gas carried in bags like embryo Zeppelins, either on the roof or in trailers; during World War Two, private cars were fitted with gas producers generating combustible gas from carbon, usually in the form of charcoal.

Serious development of alternative power sources did not begin, however, until the 1950s. Rover in Britain led the way with production of gas turbine prototypes, and both General Motors and Ford began experiments along these lines. The major American manufacturers also began looking anew at steam and electric vehicles.

Turbines failed to meet the requirements of the car industry, though they had some attraction to truck builders. Their main fault was a 'time-lag' when accelerating; also, their application to mass-produced cars depends on the development of low-cost, high-temperature components designed for satisfactory engine efficiency and performance.

Another candidate which was tried and found wanting was the Stirling 'hot-air' engine, appropriately designed by a preacher in the early 1800s. Powered by a closed-circuit system utilizing heat expansion of an inert gas, the external-combustion Stirling was at one time seriously considered by Ford as a possibility for the production cars of the late 1980s, but the programme got no further than the building of mobile test beds.

Rotary piston engines, long a fruitful field for hopeful inventors, came to the fore with the Wankel trochoidal engine pioneered by NSU in 1963, but failed to stay the course. Though rotaries are more compact than conventional reciprocating engines, they are costlier to produce and maintain, and are not so fuel-efficient.

Even the 'pollution-free' and noiseless electric car has not solved the problems which bedevilled it at the turn of the century. It still relies on heavy storage batteries with limited range, and needs to be recharged at frequent intervals. And, if its batteries are recharged from a conventional oil-fired generating station, the source of the atmospheric pollution is only

Some modern sports cars, like this 1979 Ford Mustang (1), use an exhaust-driven turbocharger for forced induction to obtain greater efficiency from a conventional petrol engine. In the mid-1960s, Ford of Britain developed a small urban electric car prototype, the Comuta (2), but shelved the project in 1967. The most commercially successful 'alternative' engine is the Wankel rotary-piston unit. This is a Citroën-built example (3). The closed-cycle Ford-Philips Stirling 'hot-air' engine (4) was tested in a Pinto car but apparently did not live up to its early promise. In Brazil in 1979, Fiat introduced the 147 saloon running on locally produced sugar cane alcohol (5), promoted by an all-girl rally team. In the summer of 1979, Californian Ken Eacrett drove his solar-powered three-wheeler (6) across the USA. Taking its power from a solar panel on the roof, the car had a 25mph top speed.

56

transferred from the car to the power station.

One of the more promising alternative power sources is the stratified-charge engine—basically a more efficient variant of the conventional petrol engine. There are two main types, the divided chamber engine and the fuel-injected stratified-charge engine.

The first type is typified by Honda's CVCC engine, which features a dual carburettor and a precombustion chamber, while Ford's PROCO ('programmed combustion') engine represents the second type. This has a special cylinder and piston head design, and uses fuel injectors to deliver a finely atomized spray of fuel directly into the combustion chamber.

But perhaps the most successful 'alternative engine' is also one of the oldest, the diesel, first devised in the 1890s. Long proven in trucks, by the late 1970s diesels were appearing in a small VW family car, the Golf. Able to run on cheaper, less volatile oil fuel than the petrol engine, and of proven longevity, the compression ignition diesel engine only suffered by comparison, as it tended to be harsher-running and less lively. However, it holds great hope for the future.

Cars of the future

WHAT SHAPE WILL TOMORROW'S car take? One thing is certain: it will not be a science-fiction fantasy vehicle powered by some revolutionary new power plant. Tomorrow's car will, in fact, be very much like today's, except that it will be far more efficient—'socially responsible' is the current in-phrase.

So far, the various alternative power sources that have been tried have all been found wanting: nothing works as well as the internal combustion engine, despite the fact that it has been around for almost a century in production cars. However, it may need to change its diet: petrol is getting scarcer and more expensive, and the prophets of doom say it may run out early in the twenty-first century. Already, new fuels are being investigated. In 1979, Saab-Finland laun-

ched a multifuel engine capable of running on fuel distilled from timber, so that the nation could aim at self-sufficiency.

The US Transportation Secretary Brock Adams called for 'the re-invention of the car', with a target of around 50 miles to the gallon for an American family car of the mid-1980s.

In Sweden, the Royal Academy of Engineering Science forecast that cars of the year 2000, despite the expected stricter anti-pollution and safety requirements, would be as roomy and comfortable as present-day models.

Their equipment, however, will be vastly more sophisticated. Volkswagen—which has declared itself committed to a piston engine for tomorrow's cars—foresees an increased use of electronic aids to driving. In-car computers,

VW predicts, will handle engine management, anti-lock braking, fault diagnosis and crash sensor equipment. By the end of the 1980s, digital displays could have replaced conventional instrument dials, and aircraft-style 'head-up read-outs' will give traffic and weather information from roadside computer links.

More efficient aerodynamics will provide dramatic fuel savings—up to 30 per cent in some cases—and both petrol and diesel engines may be turbocharged for increased efficiency. Low-weight materials will also help fuel economy—Ford-US was already testing carbon-fibre wheels in 1978.

Lighter, quieter, more fuel-efficient, more spacious—these will be the main attributes of tomorrow's car.

The 'dream cars' of the 1970s take a more thoughtful look into the future than their often bizarre predecessors of the 1950s and 1960s. Aerodynamics play a vital part in their design for an increasingly fuel-conscious world – the Ghia-styled 'Coins' of 1974 (**right**) forecast what shape the Ford sports coupé of the future might take, while the same studio's Corrida (**below**) showed how one car, in this case the Ford Fiesta, could fulfil several functions. Alfa Romeo's Eagle (**opposite**) made interesting use of digital displays instead of conventional instrumentation.

Founders of the motor industry

APPERSON, Edgar *(1870–1959)* **and Elmer** *(1861–1920)*
Collaborated with Elwood Haynes to build one of America's first cars in 1894, later forming Haynes-Apperson. After they broke with Haynes, they founded the Apperson Brothers Motor Car Company.

Herbert Austin

AUSTIN, Herbert *(1866–1941)*
Briton who worked for the Wolseley Sheep Shearing Company in Australia, then returned to England to build the first Wolseley car (1895). Left Wolseley to found Austin (1906), where landmark designs included the Seven and the 12/4. He was knighted in 1917 and became Lord Austin in 1936.

BENTLEY, Walter Owen *(1888–1971)*
Trained as a railway engineer, fitted some of the first aluminium pistons to DFP cars in 1914. After building aeroengines during World War One, he launched the Bentley car in 1919. He later worked for Lagonda.

Karl Benz

BENZ, Karl *(1844–1929)*
Began development of a petrol engine in 1878, founding Benz & Co. in 1883. Built his first motor car in 1885–86, the first petrol car conceived as a unity and owing nothing to horse-drawn carriages.

BIRKIGT, Marc *(1878–1953)*
Swiss engineer who moved to Spain, and became designer of Hispano-Suiza cars and aeroengines.

BOLLEE, Amédée *père (1844–1916)*
French bell-founder and designer of steam carriages which pioneered independent front suspension and other technical features well ahead of their time.

BOLLEE, Amédée *fils (1867–1926)*
Began with steam carriages, but turned to petrol cars in 1896, building a streamlined racer in 1899 with underslung chassis, rear-mounted twin carburettor, and four-cylinder engine with hemispherical combustion chambers.

BOLLEE, Léon *(1870–1913)*
First achieved fame with the invention of a calculating machine, then, in 1895, devised a sporting tandem-seat voiturette. In contrast, from 1903 he built refined and silent quality cars of advanced design.

BRISCOE, Benjamin *(1869–1945)*
Founded, with Jonathan Maxwell, the Maxwell-Briscoe Motor Company in 1903, and in 1910 organized the United States Motor Company, a combine of some 130 firms, which folded in 1912. In 1913 Briscoe began building cars under his own name. A visit to the 1912 London Motorcycle Show introduced him to cyclecars, which he built in France and America in conjunction with his brother Frank *(1875–1954)*.

BUGATTI, Ettore *(1881–1947)*
Born in Milan, he was designing for De Dietrich before he was 21, moved to Mathis, and in 1910 built the first Bugatti car at Molsheim (Alsace). 'Le Patron', rarely seen without his bowler hat, also affected digitated shoes.

BUICK, David Dunbar *(1855–1929)*
Applied the money he made from the invention of the enamelled bathtub to the development of a car engine with ohv. He then, in 1903, organized the Buick Motor Car Company with backing from the Briscoe brothers, but was bought out by Billy Durant late in 1904.

David Buick

CHADWICK, Lee Sherman *(1875–1958)*
Built his first car in 1899, joining Searchmont in 1900. His Chadwick company lasted from 1903 to 1911, and his racing cars pioneered the use of superchargers. His latter years were spent as the head of a stove company.

CHAPIN, Roy *(1880–1936)*
Started with Olds, then, in 1906, helped found Thomas-Detroit (later Chalmers). In 1909 he organized, along with Howard Coffin, the Hudson Motor Car Company. He was an active crusader for better roads for America.

CHAPMAN, Colin *(born 1928)*
English designer/constructor of Lotus sports and racing cars.

CHARRON, Fernand *(1866–1928)*
French cycle and car racer who collaborated (with Girardot and Voigt) in the CGV car, having made a 'killing' from holding the sole agency for Panhard-Levassor at a time of great demand. Sold his share of Charron Ltd. (as CGV became) to work for his father-in-law, Adolphe Clément, but they split up and Charron eventually built the 'Alda' car. Though he was very bald, the fashionable M. Charron rarely wore a hat, a matter for some comment at the time.

Louis Chevrolet

CHEVROLET, Louis *(1878–1941)*
Swiss racing driver who arrived in the USA in 1900 to sell a wine pump he had invented. He became a team driver for Buick and, with Etienne Planche, designed the first Chevrolet Six in 1911. He left Chevrolet to found the Frontenac Motor Company, building racing cars and 'go-faster' equipment for Model T Fords.

CHRISTIE, John Walter *(1886–1944)*
Pioneered front-wheel drive in the USA, even competing in the French Grand Prix with huge, if not particularly reliable, fwd racers. He also produced fwd tractor units for fire appliances and built an advanced tank in the 1930s.

CHRYSLER, Walter Percy *(1875–1940)*

A locomotive engineer who joined Buick in 1911, rising to become President – as well as first Vice-President of General Motors. Moved to Willys in 1920, saving this company – and Maxwell-Chalmers – from bankruptcy. He converted Maxwell into the Chrysler Corporation, acquiring Dodge in 1928.

CITROEN, André *(1878–1935)*

Frenchman who worked with Mors pre-World War One, and devised a double chevron gear which was used as the emblem of the car-producing company he founded in 1919. Development of a magnificent new factory and of the classic fwd Citroën car caused his death.

CLEMENT, Adolphe *(1855–1928)*

French cycle manufacturer who made a fortune from the French rights for the Dunlop pneumatic tyre and his exceedingly complex business dealings when he entered the motor car industry. As a result of selling the manufacturing rights to the 'Clément' car, he changed his name to 'Clément-Bayard'. His company also pioneered aeroplanes and airships.

COATALEN, Louis *(1879–1962)*

Breton engineer who came to England in 1900, working for Crowden, Humber and Hillman. His greatest designs were for Sunbeam, where he became Managing Director and built the first V-12 racing car in 1913.

CORD, Erret Lobban *(1894–1974)*

Dynamic entrepreneur who created the Auburn-Duesenberg-Cord empire, and also owned Lycoming engines, American Airlines, Stinson Aircraft and New York Shipbuilding before he was 35.

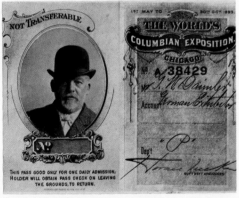

Gottlieb Daimler

DAIMLER, Gottlieb *(1834–1900)*

Born in Württemberg and trained as an engineer; becoming interested in gas engines in the 1860s, he helped develop the Otto gas engine. During the 1880s he set up on his own to develop a 'universal power source' in the shape of a light petrol engine, in collaboration with Wilhelm Maybach. This engine was fitted into a carriage in 1886, creating the first Daimler car.

DARRACQ, Alexandre *(1855–1931)*

Born in Bordeaux, Darracq entered the cycle industry in 1891, building 'Gladiator' cycles; selling out in 1896, he moved first into components, then into motor vehicles. Darracq voiturettes were particularly famous. He retired in 1912 to take a financial interest in the Deauville casino. Though Darracq built many thousands of cars, he never drove and disliked riding in them.

Georges Bouton *(left)* and Albert De Dion

DE DION, Albert *(1856–1946)*

Famous as a duellist and gambler, Comte De Dion sponsored two brothers-in-law, Bouton and Trépardoux, in the construction of steam carriages. The first practicable De Dion Bouton petrol engines appeared in 1894 and were fitted to tricycles, voiturettes (for which the marque became renowned) appearing in 1899. De Dion also founded the motoring daily *L'Auto*. He became a Marquis in 1901.

DELAGE, Louis *(1877–1947)*

French builder who supplied components to marques such as Helbe, then made complete Delage light cars from 1906. After 1919, Delage also built luxury cars.

DOBLE, Abner *(1890–1961)*

Built his first steam car in 1906, and drove a prototype to Detroit in 1914 to seek backing. Began production in San Francisco in 1920. Output was always limited, but he gained great acclaim. He later acted as a steam power consultant for overseas firms, including Sentinel steam waggons in England.

DODGE, John *(1864–1920)* and Horace *(1868–1920)*

Machinists and cycle makers, the Dodges built transmissions for Olds (1901–02), then made chassis and engines for Henry Ford in return for a tenth of his company. They sold their Ford shares for $25,000,000 and founded the Dodge Brothers company, coining the word 'dependable' to describe their products.

DUESENBERG, Frederick *(1877–1932)*

Designed his first car in 1904, and by 1913 had organized the Duesenberg Motor Company to build engines. During the 1930s Fred and his brother August built the Duesenberg luxury cars, though E. L. Cord took control of the company in 1927. Fred Duesenberg died in a car crash.

DURANT, William Crapo *(1860–1947)*

Having become a major force in the carriage industry, Billy Durant took over Buick in 1904, then, in 1908, founded the General Motors group. Ousted in 1910, by 1915 he was ready to take over again via his Chevrolet company. However, a share crash in 1920 put him out of GM again, so he established a 'Second Empire' which survived until the Depression.

DURYEA, Charles *(1861–1939)* and Frank *(1870–1967)*

In 1893 built the first practicable American car to lead to a production company, the Duryea Motor Power Wagon Company (1896).

EARL, Harley *(1893–1969)*

In the early 1920s was a director of Don Lee Corporation, which built custom coachwork for the wealthy. Became director of 'art and color' at GM in 1927, and is recognized as the first mass-production stylist. Among his styling innovations were tailfins.

S. F. Edge on a 1903 Napier

EDGE, Selwyn Francis *(1868–1940)*

Born in Sydney, New South Wales, came to England and became known as a racing cyclist. Promoted the Napier car and achieving some notable racing victories, including the only British victory in the Gordon Bennett Cup series (1902). In the 1920s, backed AC and Cubitt cars.

FLANDERS, Walter *(1871–1923)*

One of the US car industry's first mass-production experts. He was hired by Ford as production manager in 1908, but left in 1909 to found EMF. Later, he founded the United States Motor Company group.

FORD, Henry *(1863–1947)*

Son of an immigrant Irish farmer, Henry Ford wanted to lift the drudgery off farm life, and became an engineer in Detroit. In 1896 he built his first car. After two unsuccessful attempts to found manufacturing companies, he established the Ford Motor Company on June 16, 1903. He successfully defied the ALAM monopoly group.

FRANKLIN, Herbert *(1867–1956)*

Newspaper proprietor who became a pioneer of die casting, then in 1902 put the first air-cooled Franklin car on the market.

FRAZER, Joseph W. *(1894–1973)*
Having worked for Packard, GM and Pierce-Arrow, Frazer became President of Willys-Overland in 1939 and, with Henry Kaiser, founded Kaiser-Frazer in 1946 in an attempt to break the monopoly of the 'Big Three' in the popular car market.

HAYNES, Elwood G. *(1857–1925)*
Built his first car in 1894 with the help of the Apperson Brothers, and started the Haynes Automobile Company in 1898. He was also a pioneering metallurgist.

ISSIGONIS, Sir Alec *(born 1906)*
Designer of Morris Minor (1948), Mini-Minor (1959) and other fwd British Motor Corporation family cars.

JANO, Vittorio *(1891–1965)*
Italian designer for Fiat, Alfa Romeo and Lancia, for whom he created some of the finest sports and racing cars of all time.

JEFFERY, Thomas B. *(1845–1910)*
An Englishman who emigrated to the USA in 1863, and in 1879 began manufacturing 'Rambler' bicycles. He invented a 'clincher' tyre in 1891, and built his first successful car in 1900. Production of Rambler cars started in 1902.

JOHNSON, Claude *(1864–1926)*
First Secretary of the ACGBI (later the Royal Automobile Club). Introduced Rolls to Royce, and was first Managing Director of Rolls-Royce.

JORDAN, Edward *(1882–1958)*
A journalist who became Advertising Manager of the Thomas B. Jeffery Company, leaving to found the Jordan Motor Car Company in 1916. He became better known for his evocative advertising copy than for his cars.

KELSEY, Cadwallader *(1880–1970)*
Having built an experimental car in 1897, began production of Auto-Tri three-wheelers. Worked for Maxwell as Sales Manager 1905–09, then produced the Motorette car (1910–1912) and the Kelsey car (1921–1924).

KETTERING, Charles F. *(1876–1958)*
'Boss Ket' organized Delco laboratories to develop an electrical ignition system, and subsequently perfected the electric self-starter for the 1911 Cadillac. In 1920 he became head of the GM research laboratories.

KING, Charles Brady *(1868–1957)*
Built Detroit's first motor vehicle in 1896, and later designed the 'Silent Northern' and 'King 8' cars, turning to aeroengines in 1916.

LANCHESTER, Frederick *(1868–1946)*
British pioneer who built an advanced car in 1895. Apart from his contributions to automobile engineering, was one of the great pioneers of aeronautics.

LAWSON, Harry J. *(1852–1925)*
Company promotor, nicknamed 'Father of the British Motor Industry'. Attempted, from 1896, to form a patent monopoly to control the industry, and floated a number of overcapitalized companies, notably Daimler of Coventry (which survived the collapse of his empire in the early 1900s).

LEDWINKA, Hans *(1878–1967)*
Austrian designer who worked for Nesselsdorf, Steyr and Tatra, where he devised backbone chassis, all-independent suspension and air-cooled engines, latterly rear-mounted.

Hans Ledwinka

LELAND, Henry M. *(1843–1932)*
'The Master of Precision' learned his art in the arms industry. He also invented the mechanical hair-clipper and began building engines. He reorganized the Henry Ford Company as Cadillac after Ford resigned in 1902, later founding Lincoln.

LENOIR, J-J. Etienne *(1822–1900)*
A Belgian, he invented a successful method of enamelling clock faces in 1847, and in the late 1850s devised a gas engine. He built his first horseless carriage in Paris in 1862, later selling it to the Czar of Russia.

LEVASSOR, Emile *(1844–1897)*
Co-founder of Panhard-Levassor and inventor of the *Système Panhard*, in which the engine was at the front, under a bonnet, driving the rear wheels via a sliding-pinion gearbox. Died as a delayed effect of a racing accident.

MARKUS, Seigfried *(1831–1898)*
Austrian inventor who built a number of experimental internal combustion-engined test-benches from 1868. His first true car, long claimed to have been built in 1875, is now known to date from the late 1880s.

MAXWELL, Jonathan Dixon *(1864–1968)*
Starting in the cycle industry with Elmer Apperson, he worked on the 1894 Haynes-Apperson. In 1903, he joined Ben Briscoe to found the Maxwell-Briscoe company.

METZ, Charles *(1864–1937)*
Famed for his Orient cycles, Metz began production of the crude Orient Buckboard. In 1909 he introduced the low-priced friction-drive Metz 22, sold initially for home assembly.

MORRIS, William *(1877–1963)*
Starting as an Oxford cycle agent, Morris (who became Lord Nuffield) built his first Morris-Oxford light car in 1912, and came to dominate the British motor industry in the 1920s. He was renowned for his philanthropy.

NASH, Charles W. *(1864–1948)*
An itinerant farm worker, Charles Nash joined the Durant-Dort carriage company, then moved to Buick with Billy Durant, becoming President of that company in 1910 and of the whole GM group in 1912. He left to take over Jeffery and transform it into the Nash Motor Company.

OLDS, Ransom Eli *(1864–1950)*
Claimed to have built his first steam car in 1896, and his first petrol car in 1894. Success came with the 1901 Curved-Dash Oldsmobile. He later founded Reo, and also invented an early motor mower.

PENNINGTON, Edmund Joel *(1858–1911)*
American 'mechanical charlatan', who 'invented' an airship in 1885, and produced a number of eccentric motor vehicles which defied normal mechanical laws.

PEUGEOT, Armand *(1849–1915)*
Son of one of France's leading ironmongers, Peugeot translated his firm's expertise in making steel rods to replace whalebone in crinoline skirts into the manufacture of cycles. In 1889 the Peugeot company built a steam car designed by Serpollet, but then constructed tubular-framed Daimler-engined cars, France's first production cars.

POPE, Albert Augustus *(1843–1909)*
Colonel Pope founded a successful cycle manufacturing group in 1879, and moved into the motor industry via electric vehicles as early as 1896. Pope's motor group was dragged down by the decline of the cycle business.

PORSCHE, Ferdinand *(1875–1952)*
Austrian designer for Steyr, Austro-Daimler, Mercedes, Auto-Union, Cisitalia and Porsche, he created the original Volkswagen in the 1930s.

Ferdinand Porsche

PORTER, Finley Robertson *(1872–1964)*
Designed the classic Mercer Raceabout, as well as FRP and Porter cars, becoming Chief Engineer of Curtiss Aircraft in 1919.

RENAULT, Louis *(1877–1944)*
Son of a rich Parisian button maker, Louis Renault rebuilt his De Dion tricycle into a shaft-driven voiturette in 1898, and received so many orders that he began production of similar vehicles. By 1900, Renault was building 350 cars a year and was established as one of France's leading makes. Louis Renault died in prison during World War Two, having been accused of collaborating with the Germans during the Occupation of France.

RIKER, Andrew L. *(1868–1930)*
Built his first electric tricycle in 1884, but did not begin production until 1899. In 1902 joined Locomobile to design their first petrol cars.

ROESCH, Georges *(1891–1969)*
Brilliant Swiss engineer who became Chief Engineer of Clement Talbot of London at 25, designing high speed tourers of great refinement.

ROLLS, The Hon. Charles Stuart
(1877–1910)
Interested in machinery from an early age, Lord Llangottock's youngest son was a pioneer motorist and racing driver who entered the motor trade. Anxious to sell a car bearing his own name, he joined with the engineer Royce. Rolls died in a flying accident at Bournemouth, having been the first man to fly the English Channel both ways.

The Hon. C. S. Rolls (*left*) and Henry Royce

ROYCE, Henry *(1863–1933)*
Electrical engineer who built a twin-cylinder car in 1903, and went on to construct the 'best car in the world' as well as some remarkable aeroengines.

SELDEN, George Baldwin *(1846–1932)*
A patent attorney who experimented with engines from 1873 to 1875, and designed a self-propelled vehicle on which he filed a patent in 1879, the patent being granted in 1895. He sold the patent to Columbia Electric on a royalty basis in 1899, when it was used to try and create a monopoly group (Association of Licenced Automobile Manufacturers).

SERPOLLET, Léon *(1858–1907)*
Frenchman who devised the flash boiler for rapid production of steam, and built a steam tricycle in 1887. He built a number of steam three-wheelers in the 1890s, but did not seriously begin car production until the turn of the century. His sprint racers broke many speed records. His aim was to build a steamer that was as simple to control as a petrol vehicle, but his death from consumption ended the Serpollet company.

Frederick Simms

SIMMS, Frederick R. *(1863–1944)*
Brought the first Daimler engines into Britain in 1891, and fitted these power units into motor launches on the Thames. Formed the Daimler Motor Syndicate in 1893, which was taken over by Lawson interests in 1896. He invented the name 'motor-car', and helped to found the Automobile Club of Great Britain and Ireland (later the Royal Automobile Club) and the Society of Motor Manufacturers and Traders. He also built Simms cars.

SLOAN, Alfred P. *(1875–1966)*
At Durant's behest, formed the United Motors Corporation of accessory manufacturers, which was later absorbed by GM. An administrative genius, Sloan reorganized the corporate structure of GM, becoming its President from 1923–1936.

STANLEY, Francis E. *(1849–1918)* **and Freelan O.** *(1849–1940)*
The Stanley twins used the proceeds from the sale of their photographic dry-plate business to develop a steam car, the rights to which were bought for $250,000 to create Locomobile. The Stanleys came up with an improved design, Stanley steamers being built into the 1920s.

STUTZ, Harry *(1871–1930)*
Designed an improved rear axle, then became Sales Manager for Schebler carburettors, engineer for Marion and designer of the American Underslung. Manufacture of Stutz cars began in 1911; Harry Stutz resigned in 1919, later founding HCS. He was also a talented saxophonist.

THOMAS, Edwin Ross *(1850–1936)*
Though he founded the E. R. Thomas Motor Company in Buffalo, NY, in 1900 (it built the Thomas Flyer which won the round-the-world New York-Paris Race of 1908), Edwin Thomas never learned to drive.

VOISIN, Gabriel *(1880–1973)*
French aviation pioneer who went into car production between the wars with advanced and unorthodox sleeve-valve cars.

WHITE, Windsor *(1866–1958)*, **Rollin**
(1872–1968) **and Walter** *(1876–1929)*
Rollin and Windsor built the first White Steamer in 1900, and Walter was sent to London the next year to develop the European market. Rollin left the White Company (Windsor was its President) in 1914 to build Cleveland tractors, and launched the Rollin car in 1923.

WILLS, Childe Harold *(1878–1940)*
A brilliant metallurgist who helped Henry Ford develop his first cars (and also designed the famous 'Ford' script logo) and became Chief Engineer of the Ford Motor Company. He developed vanadium and molybdenum steel alloys for the motor industry. With his severance pay from Ford he founded Wills Ste Claire. In 1933 he became Chrysler's chief metallurgist.

Childe Harold Wills

WILLYS, John North *(1873–1933)*
In 1906 undertook to sell the entire output of Overland, then mounted an effort to save the company when it got into difficulties in 1907, moving production to Toledo. He built Overland production up to 95,000 units – second only to Ford – in 1915.

WINTON, Alexander *(1860–1932)*
Scots marine engineer who jumped ship in America in 1880, starting bicycle production in 1896. Built his first car in 1896, founding the Winton Motor Carriage Company next year. In 1903, he launched an eight-cylinder 'Bullet' racer. His designs featured pneumatic controls. When car production was suspended in 1924, he began manufacture of diesel engines.

1914 Prince Henry Vauxhall

TRUCKS & BUSES

DENIS MILLER

An idea is born

THE MAN generally credited with developing the world's first practical self-propelled vehicle in 1769 is Captain Nicolas Joseph Cugnot, of the Artillerie Française, although there were numerous other experiments prior to this time. The earliest recorded attempt was made by the German, Johann Hautach, who, in the sixteenth century, constructed a horseless carriage apparently propelled by a system of coiled springs. One century later, two Englishmen, Ramsay and Wildgoose, patented another design. Both types were purely experimental, however, and it is unlikely that they ever ran on a public highway.

Cugnot worked hard, first building a model steam carriage to illustrate his ideas. The French government was favourably impressed and ordered him to construct a full-size model, which was demonstrated in front of the French Minister of War. Although the demonstration proved that the design was not quite as reliable as it could have been, a second machine was ordered with a 4¹/₂-ton payload capable of hauling field artillery on level ground at a speed of 6km/h. In spite of being crude and clumsy, this vehicle was a comparative success.

In 1784, while working for the Cornish steam engine manufacturers Boulton and Watt, William Murdock, a young Scottish mechanic, built his first steam carriage, but this was not particularly successful, and again appears never to have run on the public highway. Meanwhile, Oliver Evans, a Welsh inventor living in the United States, was investigating the possibility of applying steam power to a road-going carriage, and in 1787 was granted the exclusive right to develop such a machine in the State of Maryland. No actual wagon appears to have materialized, although in 1804 he fitted wheels to a 20-ton steam dredger and drove it under its own power to the River Schuylkill, along which he sailed to Delaware. This was undoubtedly the world's first self-propelled amphibious vehicle, and Evans's ideas also formed the first US patent for a self-propelled steam road vehicle in 1789. A year later, Charles Dalley, of Amiens, France, constructed a rela-

Above The world's oldest surviving self-propelled vehicle is Cugnot's 1770 artillery tractor. *Left* In 1833 Dr F. Church designed a very ornate machine, which even had springs supporting the simple front wheel. *Opposite left* One year after the success of Trevithick's first self-propelled steam carriage in 1801, he constructed a new model *Opposite top right* This replica of William Murdock's steam vehicle of 1784 shows steam propulsion at its simplest. *Opposite bottom right* Goldsworthy steam carriages were reminiscent of the stage coach, this example was used on Sir Charles Dance's Gloucester-Cheltenham run.

tively successful steam carriage, while in America both Apollo Kinsley of Hartford, Connecticut, and Nathan Read, of Eden, Massachusetts, developed vehicles of this type.

In the United Kingdom, Richard Trevithick, who already held the distinction of building the world's first steam railway locomotive, constructed the world's first self-propelled steam carriage to run successfully on public roads. It appeared in 1801. One year later Trevithick's second steam carriage was completed, but lack of finance curtailed further development. It was the lack of funds which also hampered other early experiments in the field, particularly in the United Kingdom, where many financiers already had a vested interest in other forms of transport, such as canals and railways, and were unlikely to show

much enthusiasm for a competitive activity. It may well have been this lack of financial backing that led to an economy of design which precipitated serious, and often fatal, accidents involving early self-propelled vehicles such as boiler explosions, and steering and brake failures, none of which did anything to instil enthusiasm for this new mode of transport.

Goldsworthy Gurney was quick to realize that safety had to come first if the public was to have any confidence in mechanical road transport, and by 1827, following experiments with three alternative types of boiler, he had constructed his first steam coach. Having perfected a "safe" boiler, he then looked for other improvements, deciding to use coke, which was smokeless, for fuel, rather than coal. Within a year he had perfected his de-

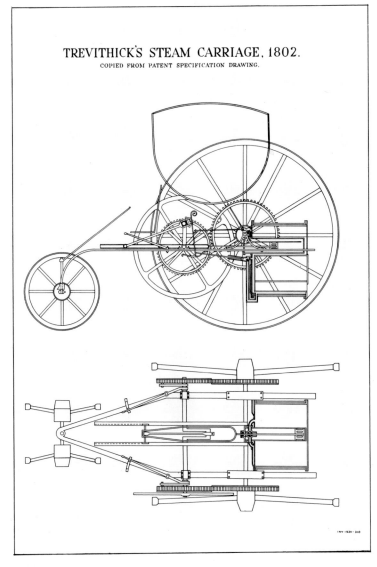

TREVITHICK'S STEAM CARRIAGE, 1802.
COPIED FROM PATENT SPECIFICATION DRAWING.

sign with one machine completing a 135-km run between Melksham, Wilts, and Cranford, Middx, in just ten hours. Sir Charles Dance was a Gurney customer who improved the specification still further and, in 1831, inaugurated a service which ran four times a day along a 14-km route between Gloucester and Cheltenham at an average speed, including stops, of 16 to 19km/h. Other routes followed, but both official and unofficial opposition forced him to close down.

One of the most successful of all United Kingdom steam carriage builders was Walter Hancock, who built his first machine in 1827. Again, safety was of prime consideration, and the first Hancock coach embodied a chain transmission and tight metal boiler joints to withstand high pressures. In 1828 the French engineer

Onesiphore Pecqueur designed and patented a 4-ton steam truck, but construction is not recorded.

Opposition to steam-powered road vehicles in the United Kingdom grew rapidly, with many influential people being against the project. As a result, in 1831 a series of prohibitive bills were passed by the British government to discourage the development of steam vehicles.

The world's first automotive publication, *The Journal of Elemental Locomotion*, was founded by Alexander Gordon in 1832. Sir Goldsworthy Gurney did much to reverse the government's attitude and an attempt was made to form the United Kingdom's first public passenger transport company. This was the London, Holyhead & Liverpool Steam Coach & Road Co, with a capital of £350,000.

Although it failed, at least the company showed the country's growing awareness of the commercial possibilities of mechanical road transport.

As a result of these moves by the government, the development of steam road propulsion stagnated for thirty years, during which time many pioneers turned to the railways and steam shipping.

While the development of self-propelled road vehicles had been largely halted, there were numerous developments on the agricultural front, where portable steam engines, previously hauled by horses, were now being converted to self-propulsion.

By the 1850s, some of the more intrepid inventors were again looking at road vehicles and, despite their being illegal in the United Kingdom, demonstrations frequently took place on

the public highways. This unfortunately led to the crippling Locomotive Acts of 1861 and 1865, and to the Highways & Locomotives (Amendment) Act of 1878. Thus, as Continental and American inventors raced ahead, so their British counterparts were left behind.

While this was taking place in the United Kingdom, in France, Joseph Ravel had taken out a patent in 1868 for "a steam generator heated by mineral oils supplied to steam locomotives on ordinary roads and to all industrial purposes", which was later developed into a petroleum-fuelled steamer. An Englishman, Joseph Wilkinson, is also said to have developed such a system and J H Knight, of Farnham, Surrey, had built a 1½-ton steam carriage. Another French development was the gas engine invented by Etienne Lenoir in 1860, in which gas was mixed with air and ignited by electricity. This was used in the inventor's first horseless carriage two years later. By 1872 the first engine to use fuel oil rather than gas was patented in the United Kingdom by George Brayton, and three years later what may have been the world's first self-propelled load-carrier was created – a 4-ton steam wagon constructed by Brown & May, of Devizes, Wilts. Unfortunately, Brayton's idea was developed into designs for a complete vehicle by George Baldwin Selden, Rochester, New York, in 1879 and led ultimately to a US patent being granted in 1895, in which anyone else using an internal-combustion engine in a road vehicle had to pay royalties to Selden. This arrangement held until 1911 and did much to stunt motor industry growth in the United States.

However, the greatest advances were about to be made in Germany, and were to be crucial to the development of heavy trucks and buses.

Karl Benz was the son of an engine driver, and attended an engineering course at the Karlsruhe Polytechnic before joining a local railway locomotive builder. He became fascinated with the theories of Professor Redtenbacher at the Polytechnic, and as a result turned his attention to the development of the internal-combus-

tion engine for road vehicles. Soon Benz had set up his own business, as a manufacturer of stationary gas engines and in 1885, at his Mannheim premises, his first motor car, a 3-wheeler, began to take shape. This was the world's first internal-combustion engined passenger car and set numerous precedents for the future. Drive was transmitted to a countershaft and then by chain and sprocket to the rear wheels, while other features included liquid cooling and an electric ignition system.

Another German pioneer was Gottlieb Daimler, who worked in many parts of Europe before settling in Germany and developing oil engines with Dr Nickolaus August Otto and Eugen Langen. Neither of the latter saw much future in the use of the internal-

combustion engine to provide power for road vehicles, so, in 1882, Daimler resigned and was joined at an experimental workshop in Cannstatt by Wilhelm Maybach, another ex-employee of Otto and Langen. Their first gas engine was a single-cyl air-cooled horizontal unit which was followed, in 1883, by a fully-enclosed design with tube ignition which, by 1885, was being used to power a motorized bicycle. Daimler's first car appeared in 1886. This was a converted horse-drawn carriage powered by a 1½hp single-cyl air-cooled unit with 2-speed transmission via a friction clutch to the rear wheels. An improved model, with differential gear and a 4-speed transmission, appeared in 1889, this having a rear-mounted single-cyl vertical water-cooled engine and all-gear final

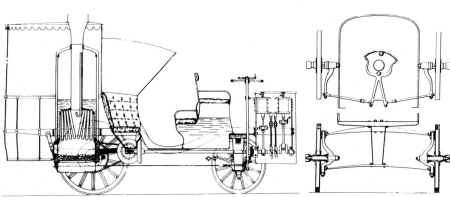

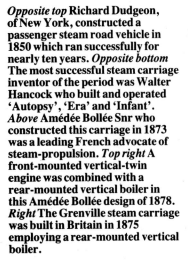

Opposite top Richard Dudgeon, of New York, constructed a passenger steam road vehicle in 1850 which ran successfully for nearly ten years. *Opposite bottom* The most successful steam carriage inventor of the period was Walter Hancock who built and operated 'Autopsy', 'Era' and 'Infant'. *Above* Amédée Bollée Snr who constructed this carriage in 1873 was a leading French advocate of steam-propulsion. *Top right* A front-mounted vertical-twin engine was combined with a rear-mounted vertical boiler in this Amédée Bollée design of 1878. *Right* The Grenville steam carriage was built in Britain in 1875 employing a rear-mounted vertical boiler.

drive. Daimler's third attempt incorporated belt transmission and a 'V'-twin engine, and was one of the most important landmarks in the early days of motoring. Simultaneously, Benz was improving his self-propelled 3-wheeler, but it was in 1891 that his first 4-wheeled passenger car was built.

While these ideas were taking shape in Germany, the French were also hard at work. In 1890 Léon Serpollet took a significant step in the development of steam propulsion for road vehicles by inventing the "flash" boiler. Meanwhile, Panhard et Levassor, Paris, which had been appointed an agent for Daimler gas and oil engines, was soon developing in 1891 the world's first "real" passenger car, using a ladder-type chassis frame and full working drawings. Powered by a 'V'-twin Daimler engine mounted vertically at the front, this had a clutch and sliding 3-speed pinion transmission and marked the dawn of the motor car.

The first self-propelled vehicle to be exported from the United States was a steam carriage built by R E Olds which was delivered to the Francis Times Co, Bombay, India. In the United Kingdom, Hornsby & Son developed its first oil engine the following year. The Germans, however, were in the forefront of internal-combustion engine developments, and were now regularly supplying such units to other road vehicle builders throughout the Western world.

For the time being, however, Maurice LeBlant's 1892 steam vans, with Serpollet boilers and 3-cyl engines with steersman at the front and stoker at the rear, were about the only self-propelled load-carriers in Europe. One was entered in the world's first motor vehicle trial between Paris and Rouen in 1894, but was only marginally successful. Also in 1894, an experimental 5-ton steam wagon was built at Leyland, Lancs, by the young James Sumner, forming the foundations of the world-renowned commercial vehicle manufacturer, Leyland Vehicles.

The first light commercials were also French, derived from Panhard et Levassor and Peugeot passenger car designs and there were also battery-electric types such as those built by Jeantaud and Krieger. The next two years, however, were to see the dawn of the internal-combustion engined commercial vehicle.

Fire engines

The lure of the fire engine is universal. From small boys to grown men, the sound of the siren stops all in their tracks just as the clanging bell and clattering hooves did at the turn of the century. When originally developed, the fire engine was a means of combating fire but can now handle a multitude of diverse tasks the most important of which is rescue. Thus, a host of special machinery has been designed, often mounted on specially developed reliable chassis capable of high-speed operation. While many truck manufacturers have, from time to time, offered a fire engine chassis, it is the specialist companies such as American LaFrance, Dennis, Merryweather, Seagrave and Ward LaFrance that have become world famous in this field.

1 In 1903 Merryweather & Sons Ltd supplied the world's first petrol-engined chemical appliance to the Tottenham Fire Brigade.
2 The Dependable Truck & Tractor Co, Illinois, built this chemical appliance around 1921.
3 As early as 1907, Gobron-Brillié had combined a petrol-engined chassis with a steam-powered pump. 4 The Dennis was the most popular British appliance of the 1920s and 30s. 5 In 1952 the Dennis F8 appliance appeared. It was used as a motor pump. 6 This American LaFrance has an artic aerial ladder truck.
7 Comparatively rare as a fire appliance, this Bedford RMA was fitted with a hydraulic watertower.
8 In 1977 the 6x6 Oshkosh 'M'-Series was launched for special use on airfields.
9 Daimler-Benz offers the 4x4 Unimags with chemical foam equipment for industrial use.
10 The White 'Road Xpeditor 2'.

The experimental years

HORSELESS CARRIAGE FEVER was now rife throughout Europe, the United States, and the United Kingdom. By the mid-1890s there were many entrepreneurs in road vehicle development, but one man in particular got things underway in the United Kingdom. He was Sir David Salomons who, as a skilled engineer and Mayor of Tunbridge Wells, Kent, organized what was probably the world's first horseless carriage exhibition, on the Tunbridge Wells Agricultural Showground in 1895. Although only five vehicles (including a Daimler-engined Panhard et Levassor motor fire pump and a De Dion-Bouton "steam horse") were present, the event attracted much attention.

One month later, the inaugural meeting of the Self-Propelled Traffic Association (SPTA) was held in London, again organized by Sir David, but with the assistance of Frederick Richard Simms, another motoring pioneer who was a director of Daimler Motoren Gesellschaft. He had been responsible for establishing Daimler products in the United Kingdom and had developed an automatic fuel feed system for carburettors. The idea behind the SPTA was to put pressure on the government to repeal the Highways & Locomotives (Amendment) Act of 1878, in order to clear the way for new developments in the automotive field. A deputation was to meet the President of the Board of Agriculture.

With restrictions still in force, there was little hope for the British motor industry, whereas on the Continent, inventors were moving ahead with revolutionary ideas. Some of these were quickly taken up by manufacturers in other countries. Richard F Stewart, New York, United States, for example, used a 2hp Daimler engine and internal-gear drive in his prototype 1895 wagon.

As a prelude to the repeal of the 1878 Act, the Daimler Motor Co was registered in England early in 1896. Chairman was Harry J Lawson, and other directors included such notables as the Hon Evelyn Ellis, Gottlieb Daimler, William Wright, Henry Sturmey, J H Mace, H E Sherwin

Holt and J S Bradshaw. Frederick Simms was Consulting Engineer and J S Critchley was Works Manager. The new company acquired a disused cotton mill in Coventry and was soon in business as the United Kingdom's first motor manufacturer. Lawson also set up the Great Horseless Carriage Co and organized a petition to the House of Commons requesting that the 1878 Act be repealed.

Another Lawson enterprise was the formation of the Motor Car Club (MCC), which was described as "a society for the protection, encourage-

ment and development of the motor car industry". However, it is more likely that it was set up to serve its founder's own ends. One of the first tasks of the MCC was to put on an exhibition of horseless carriages at London's Imperial Institute, opening to the public in May 1896. Every conceivable type of vehicle was present, including a Peugeot-built Daimler bus. While this event was in progress, a Bill repealing the 1878 Act was in preparation.

One of the first production load-carriers in the United States was a pe-

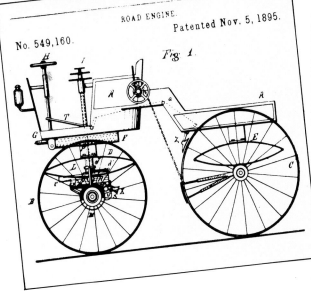

Far left John I Thornycroft's 1-ton steam van had front-wheel drive and near wheel steer layout. *Left and above* Selden's steam vehicle which was constructed in the 1870s. In spite of this, it was not patented until 1895 and the patent was worded in such a way that it held back US motor industry development until 1911.

trol-engined wagon entered by the Langert Co, Philadelphia, Pennsylvania, in the 1896 Cosmopolitan Race from New York to Irvington-on-the-Hudson and back. At the same time, a horse-drawn van was converted into a steam wagon by the Cruickshank Engineering Works, Providence, Rhode Island; Charles Woods, Chicago, was alleged to have built the first practical battery-electric commercial; and C S Fairfield, Portland, Oregon, built a kerosene-engined passenger model. In Germany, Daimler Motoren Gesellschaft had built the first purpose-built Daimler truck – a 2-tonner which, like the company's passenger cars, had the driver at the front and engine at the rear.

The 1878 Act was withdrawn with the introduction of the Locomotives on Highways Act in 1896. This stipulated the speeds at which vehicles could travel. This also stipulated that motor vehicles weighing up to 1½ tons unladen could now travel at up to 18km/h, those weighing between 1½ and 2 tons could travel at up to 12km/h and any vehicle exceeding 2 tons was restricted to 7km/h.

The first commercial load-carrying vehicle in the United Kingdom was a 1-ton steam van with front-wheel drive and rear-wheel steering built by John Isaac Thornycroft, Chiswick, West London. Powered by a Strickland vertical twin marine engine, this was shown at the 1896 Crystal Palace Motor Show organized by Sir David Salomons. It was quickly followed by a 1½-ton steamer built by the Lancashire Steam Motor Co, successor to James Sumner's small business in Leyland, Lancs. In Germany, meanwhile, the Daimler internal-combustion en-

Above **By 1898 German Daimler trucks had adapted a front-engined layout and they had a tube radiator and pinion drive.**
Right **Completed in 1898, just in time for the Liverpool Heavy Vehicle Trials, this Thornycroft was the world's first artic steam lorry.**

gined truck range was being expanded to include models from 1½ to 5 tons capacity with power outputs of up to 10hp.

Petrol, diesel or steam?

ALTHOUGH REGARDED as a modern means of propulsion, the pioneer work of the diesel was undertaken at the turn of the century, when "heavy" loads were moved by steam. The 1½-ton steam wagon built by the Lancashire Steam Motor Co in 1896 won a Silver Medal at the Royal Agricultural Society's Manchester Trials in 1897. Later that year, the first petrol-engined commercial to be sold in the United Kingdom was a Daimler. At about the same time, MAN of Germany announced the world's first heavy oil engine, and before the end of the year, Daimler adopted a front-engined layout for all commercial models, with the driver positioned on top to provide greater load-carrying area than bonneted types of the same wheelbase. This layout was also used by other manufacturers in the years leading up to 1900, although Daimler himself settled on the bonneted style in 1899, following driver complaints of excessive vibration and difficulty in reaching the vehicle's lofty perch.

In 1898 the American inventor Alexander Winton introduced the first United States petrol-engined load-carrier built in any quantity. A L Riker perfected his design for a series of heavy battery-electric commercials, exemplified by a 1315-kg payload vehicle propelled by batteries weighing 45,359kg, which he exhibited at Madison Square Gardens. It was in the United States that the battery-electric commercial was to have its greatest following during these formative years.

In Germany, Daimler had started to use Bosch magneto ignitions, developed jointly by Robert Bosch and Frederick Simms, which began to woo customers away from steam propulsion. This movement did not, how-

Left One of London's first motor-buses was a vulgar-looking Daimler that ran between Oxford Circus and South Kensington. *Below left* Built in 1902, this 3-ton Thornycroft steamer had a vertical water-tube boiler and a compound "undertype" engine. *Below* This steam-powered mail van was shipped to Ceylon in 1901. It was the Lancashire Steam Motor Co's first export order.

THORNYCROFT

ROYAL MAIL

ever, apply to the American market, where oil was plentiful and steam had never figured greatly.

Prompted by the repeal of the 1878 Act, the Liverpool Branch of the Self-Propelled Traffic Association, by then affiliated to the Automobile Club of Great Britain and Ireland, organized the first of a series of heavy vehicle trials in 1898, the second taking place in 1899 and the third in 1901. These were held at the instigation of the Liverpool Branch's Honorary Secretary, Mr E Shrapnell-Smith, a great enthusiast for mechanical commercial transport, who succeeded in his wish of encouraging the manufacture of such vehicles.

By 1899 Thornycroft's steam wagons were becoming popular as tippers and refuse collectors, as well as seeing active service in the Boer War. The same company had also completed work on the world's first steam-powered articulated lorry. Generally, however, there was no standard mode of propulsion, the choice ranging through steam, petrol, kerosene and electricity.

The heavy oil or diesel engine should not be forgotten, as eventually it would become almost universally accepted for use in heavy commercials. Despite Rudolf Diesel's pioneering work in Germany (his main achievement being the development

of an automatic ignition system using compressed air) it was two Englishmen, Priestman and Ackroyd Stuart, who developed the heavy oil engine as we know it today. Priestman adopted a system whereby fuel was injected into a cylinder-held pocket of air at maximum pressure and he had the world's first oil-engined lorry on the road by 1897. Meanwhile, Ackroyd Stuart developed the hot bulb ignition system, which replaced the external method used by Priestman and others.

Steam vehicles excepted, commercial load-carrying development paralleled that of the passenger car, which was more noticeable in the lighter designs. Steamers were especially popular in the United Kingdom, where plentiful supplies of comparatively cheap coal and coke were readily available. Such machines were normally of "undertype" layout, with engine slung beneath the chassis frame and a vertical boiler located ahead of, or behind, the driver, thereby providing maximum load space. Engine accessibility was poor, and boilers were often inefficient, but the solutions to these problems were to be found in the United Kingdom by 1901.

The last year of the nineteenth century saw some bus operators experimenting with self-propelled vehicles, but it was still to be some time before these ousted the ever-faithful horse. From 1900 onwards, however, the development of the self-propelled commercial load-carrier was to become even more fascinating than that of the passenger motor car.

The truck revolution

THE COMMERCIAL VEHICLE was by no means a European idea, because it was at this time that the United States began vehicle trials, thereby increasing the interest in such vehicles in the country.

With the turn of the century, the internal-combustion engine had yet to prove itself. Unreliability continued to be a major obstacle to commercial acceptance and business people generally regarded it as more for the mad motoring public than as being reliable for goods delivery. Horse-drawn or steam vehicles were accepted as the ideal choice for work of this nature. In an attempt to counteract this attitude and establish the internal-combustion engined vehicle in business circles, the British Automobile Club set up the Motor Van, Wagon & Omnibus Users' Association, which subsequently provided much of the impetus required.

By 1900 Daimler had built the world's first charabanc, and the German Army was undertaking field trials with a Daimler lorry. In 1901 the world's first mechanical street sweeper was built by the American, John Collins, of Connecticut, and an American subsidiary of the German

Top Leyland Motors Ltd received one of the first Royal Warrants granted to a British Motor manufacturer for a shooting van which they built in 1910 for King George V. The warrant is shown above the van together with the Leyland logo. *Above* Affectionately known as "The Pig", the first petrol-engined Leyland was a 1½-ton truck. *Left* While petrol-engined vehicles were now dealing with the lighter loads, a 6 ton steamer, such as this Leyland, was used for larger consignments.

Right The Manhattan sight-seeing bus of 1904 was one of the earliest production vehicles built in the United States by the Mack brothers. *Above* By 1910 Reliant trucks were reaching the end of the line as a marque in their own right, having already been taken over by General Motors. *Below* Early Daimler ideas were now being reflected in other marques such as this three ton Bussing made in 1902.

Daimler organization set up what is believed to have been the world's first truck service and tow-in scheme. On the steam front, the British firm of Fodens Ltd introduced the efficient loco-type horizontal boiler and "over-type" engine on a new wagon, which was quickly copied, despite the fact that it occupied more load space. In 1902 the first petrol-engined Thornycroft commercial appeared, a 2-ton lorry, relying upon experience gained from the manufacture of internal-combustion engined passenger cars. This company did not forsake its steam wagons, and later developed a demountable body system for its municipal steamers. In 1904, the John S Muir Syndicate announced a steam-powered sweeper/sprinkler which was another first in the municipal field.

America's first truck contest was organized in May 1903 by the newly formed Automobile Club of America, using a two-stage course starting from the club's headquarters in New York's Fifth Avenue. It was a two-day event, with entries divided into two classes, delivery wagons and heavy trucks, the former having to complete 64km a day and the latter 48km. All entries had to be fully laden, the winners on both days being a Knox-Waterless and a Herschmann steamer. As in the United Kingdom, this event encouraged the growth of vehicle manufacture. A specialist journal, *The Horseless Age,* commented that delivery wagons had now "arrived".

On the passenger vehicle scene, London witnessed numerous experiments with mechanically-propelled vehicles of this type, many being steam-powered and a frightening experience to the many horse-drawn vehicles still in operation. The first fleet of self-propelled buses to be used appears to have been that of the London General Omnibus Co, which had a number of vehicles in service by 1904. Among early experiments were those of the London Road Car Co, which introduced a few Maudslay buses as early as 1902. The Maudslay Motor Co Ltd, Coventry, was a pioneer in the development of the British commercial vehicle industry, using many advanced features in its designs.

One such was the single-piece axle; another was removable inspection plates in the engine crankcase to facilitate big-end inspection and the removal of damaged connecting rods or pistons.

By this time, United Kingdom speed restrictions had been relaxed and the Lancashire Steam Motor Co announced its first internal-combustion engined commercial – a 1½-ton model affectionately known as "The Pig". A new type of passenger vehicle which became popular at this time was the charabanc, with each row of seats being slightly higher than the one in front, to provide all passengers with a good view of the road ahead. Until the passenger car became a viable proposition for the working classes, the charabanc took pride of place in many fleets, particularly those based in coastal and tourist areas.

On the other side of the Atlantic, another commercial vehicle test was held in New York in April 1904, to encourage more firms to build such vehicles. Many were of driver-over-engine layout, as in the case of the first Daimlers, and by the end of 1904 the first power-assisted steering system had been developed. A year later petrol-engined buses ran for the first time on New York's fashionable Fifth Avenue.

For city deliveries, the heavy battery-electric wagon was coming into its own but was restricted to a particular operating base, where its batteries could be re-charged. The battery-electric had both advantages and disadvantages. One advantage was that it was comparatively easy to maintain, while, on the negative side, the batteries were exceptionally heavy – until Thomas Edison discovered the iron-nickel-alkaline battery in 1908. Such machines were also ponderously slow, often necessitating the use of two or even four traction motors, usually mounted in the vehicle's wheels.

In the United Kingdom, in March 1905, the first edition of *Commercial Motor* appeared (later to become one of the most important heavy automotive journals in the world) with E Shrapnell-Smith as Editor, joined three months later by *Motor Traction*.

The trade paper 'The Commercial Motor' first came out on 16 March, 1905. It was priced at one penny and included advertisements for truck parts as well as for trucks.

Top left The VCPL bus was unique in having two engines slung beneath the vehicle. Each of these engines supplied current to an electric motor at each rear wheel. *Next row extreme left* C A Tilt's first truck, a 1½-ton Diamond T which he built in 1911. He quickly introduced other models with capacities up to 5 tons. *Left* This 5-ton "overtype" wagon was a rarity, built by "undertype" pioneer Alley and McLellon Ltd. *Below and bottom* While Adolph Saurer AG, Switzerland was exporting ambulances to Russia, a plant was being set up in the USA and a US-built 4-tonner was sent on a transcontinental publicity run. The Saurer logo is shown to the right of the picture.

Meanwhile, in Lavender Hill, South London, Commercial Motors Ltd had been set up to pursue the commercial possibilities of the Linley pre-select gearbox. A 4-ton iron-wheeled lorry called the CC was constructed, which was to become the Commer. The development of the new transmission systems occupied a great deal of thought at this time. Some, such as Panhard, used a sliding-tooth system, and others, such as DeDion, left the gears in mesh, with gear-changing effected by the use of expanding friction clutches. There were also planetary or constant-mesh systems, and the German inventor, Dr H Föttinger, even developed an automatic system.

The first American motor truck show was held in Chicago in 1907, and the world's first steam vacuum cesspool emptier, developed by Merryweather & Sons Ltd, appeared in 1908. The latter made the self-propelled vehicle more important than it had been in local authorities. The Chicago event attracted attention on both sides of the Atlantic, due to the publicity surrounding a 489-km test run accomplished by a 3-ton petrol-engined Reliance in less than four days. A 1609-km commercial vehicle trial for 19 petrol-engined 3-tonners and 10 petrol- and steam-powered 5-tonners was organized by the Automobile Club in 1907. The first British Commercial Motor Show was held at Olympia, London, in the same year, under the jurisdiction of the Society of Motor Manufacturers & Traders. These events finally set the commercial vehicle on the map.

Some manufacturers were now turning from steam to petrol, although few completely abandoned the former. Thus, the Lancashire Steam Motor Co became Leyland Motors Ltd, and two petrol-engined lorries were the first internal-combustion engined Thornycrofts to receive a War Office diploma. The Swiss Saurer company was now converting 4-cyl Safir petrol engines into diesel units, and developed an engine brake which compressed air inside the engine, converting it into a retarder. This same company was soon exporting petrol-engined trucks worldwide. Other sig-

nificant advances included the first closed-top double-deck bus and trolleybus experiments were held in North London.

Elsewhere, the first production articulated lorry was seen, namely the unusual 3-wheeled Knox, built in Springfield, Massachusetts, United States. A major development of 1909 was Sven Winquist's ball-race system for commercial vehicle wheels, successfully tested in a new Scania truck between Malmo and Stockholm in Sweden.

The London General Omnibus Co Ltd (LGOC) had meanwhile been busy acquiring various independent operators, but was finding its motley collection of self-propelled buses

none too reliable. Accordingly, the Associated Equipment Co, which was responsible for the LGOC's maintenance facilities, began constructing its own vehicles in Walthamstow. The first was the AEC 'X'-Type, followed before the end of 1910 by the most advanced open-top double-decker seen so far – the famous 'B'-Type with ultra-lightweight chassis and body, conforming to police regulations limiting the gross weight to 3½ tons. Instead of the more popular channel-steel frame, the 'B'-Type was of ash wood with nickel-steel flitch plates, apparently used to counteract vibration.

Another model which was gaining popularity was the Tilling-Stevens pe-

Top left The 24-seat Thames coach, resembling a motorized stage coach, was another oddity of the pre-World War II days. *Far left top* George A Brockway's first truck was this bonneted high-wheeler, a design typical of many US manufacturers of the period. *Far left bottom* The Reo 'Democrat' wagon introduced in 1911 by R E Old's Reo Motor Car Co was another vehicle which followed the high-wheeler principle. *Left* The LGOC's 'B'-Type double decker revolutionized London's public transport system and during the war it provided transport to the Front. *Right* Despite the general acceptance of a bonneted layout, there were still a few strange designs around in 1911 when this French Berliet 'CAT'-Type was built.

trol-electric, which eliminated gear-changing, making a driver's transition from horse to internal-combustion driving that much easier. Another vehicle which used a similar system was the KPL, built by the Daimler Motor Co Ltd, Coventry. This was even more revolutionary, being of integral construction with two Knight sleeve-valve petrol engines coupled to two traction motors which, in turn, were connected to each rear wheel. Four-wheel brakes were another unusual feature.

Following the country's first War Department vehicle trials, Britain's first "subsidy" scheme was devised, whereby an operator buying a lorry conforming to a particular specifica-tion was entitled to an annual subsidy of £110, provided the vehicle was available to the military authorities, within 72 hours, in an emergency. By 1911 both Leeds and Bradford were running the first British trolleybus fleets. The "subsidy" scheme did much to establish conformity amongst British vehicle manufacturers.

The world's first tiltcab truck was the American-built Pope-Hartford of 1912, and in 1913 an even more unusual design, the 2/3-ton Austin twin-shaft lorry, was announced. The inauguration of the world's first true motor truck assembly line at the Ford Motor Co plant, Dearborn, Michigan, took place in 1914, resulting in the United States becoming a world lead-er in truck production. Meanwhile, Sydney Guy, formerly of Sunbeam, unveiled his first commercial, a 1½-ton design with one of the first over-drive transmissions, a road speed governor and, even rarer, detachable overhead valves.

By the time World War I broke out, there had been many other advances in the commercial vehicle field. Steam wagons, for example, were now shod with solid rubber tyres instead of the noisy steel units fitted to earlier models, and internal-combustion engined commercials were rapidly replacing the horse. New bus services were being established in most countries and, because of the competitiveness of operators, advances were rapid.

Buses

Road passenger transport in the early 1900s was undertaken by goods chassis fitted with passenger-carrying bodies. Bus services were maintained by single- and double-deckers, the latter open-topped, with very high floor levels and it was not unusual for some operators to run a single chassis with two bodies – one for goods, the other for passengers. By the 1920s this attitude was changing and lower-loading passenger chassis were appearing. Greater comfort came about through the introduction of pneumatic tyres, covering in top decks and general weather-proofing of bus bodies, while developments of the 1930s brought about greater carrying capacities through the use of multi axles. Chassisless and even articulated types now prevail.

The bus is the workhorse of the road passenger transport industry and the coach is its somewhat upstage sister, with more luxurious accommodation and often capable of higher speeds. The first true coaches were the toastracks and charabancs of the pre World War I era. These were invariably trucks during the week but rebodied at weekends to take parties of trippers to the coast. Many firms up to the 1950s built both buses and coaches, some have since specialised in one or the other and certain European manufacturers are now renowned for their coach models.

1 The earliest motorbuses followed German designs, this open-topped bus, of c.1914, was a British-built Daimler. 2 A Tilling-Stevens with petrol-electric transmission. 3 Glasgow Corporation took delivery of its first batch of BUT single-deck trolleybuses around 1953. These were unique to Glasgow and had 36-seat centre-entrance standee bodies. 4 LGOC brought in their S-Type, a 54-seat double decker bus which they launched on London. 5 This Bristol K5G was originally delivered to the Hants and Dorset Motor Services Ltd in 1940. In 1954 it was rebodied and used as an open-topper sea front bus. 6 These 1948 MCI 'Courier' single-deckers lined up at Windsor, Ontario, were typical of North American and Canadian passenger models of the late 1940s and early '50s. 7 The first two Birmingham-built Metrobuses to be used in London ran on the number 16 route between Cricklewood Garage and Victoria. 8 The most common Swiss postal coach was the Saurer. For many years the postal coach was unique to Switzerland but it is now familiar in a number of countries. 9 This Leyland 'Tiger Cub' operated by Watt Bros City Coast Buses, Queensland, Australia is similar to the MCI Courier.

The great war

AN IMMEDIATE DEMAND for mechanical military transport following the declaration of war in Europe was partly solved by a considerable influx of well-engineered cross-country trucks from the United States. Those countries that had prepared in advance by introducing "subsidy" schemes soon found they were in a far superior position to those that had not. Despite this, problems abounded.

Steam-powered vehicles such as traction engines had been used on a small scale in earlier situations, but the internal-combustion engined truck had never been used in war conditions, and weaknesses in design were soon apparent. These included insufficient power, lack of ground clearance, and poor protection of mechanical units from the ravages of water and mud, for which the Flanders battlefields were soon renowned. There was, however, another major problem that few had foreseen. Both sides in the conflict used many components supplied by firms on the opposing side: German-manufactured Bosch magnetos were used almost exclusively by the Allies, while German forces relied largely upon British- and

French-manufactured Dunlop and Michelin tyres. Luckily, the Bosch magneto had been developed jointly by Robert Bosch and the American Frederick Simms, and German supplies were replaced by magnetos from the Simms Magneto Co factory, Watsersing, New Jersey.

At this stage it is worth looking in depth at some of the "subsidy" schemes operating at the time. The instigators of this idea were the Germans who, in the years prior to 1914, had been building up their military reserves. The German scheme is understood to have applied to any truck which an operator was prepared to release to the military upon mobilization. The operator received an initial grant of £150 towards the purchase of the vehicle, followed by a subsidy of £60 for each of the next four years. By the time war was declared, some 825 "subsidy" trucks had been released to the German Armed Forces.

A similar scheme was organized by the French government, and the British system, in which there were two classes of load-carrying vehicle – a 1½-tonner and a 3-tonner – brought about the first signs of standardization in the

Above Leyland's 'RAF'-Type 3-tonner was one of the best known British 'subsidy' types. *Right* After the war many of these vehicles were resold onto the civilian market, like this Chivers' van.

Left Many ''Tommies'', such as these members of the 2nd Battalion Royal Warwickshire Regiment, made their last journeys in London's 'B'-Type buses. *Below* Many British industries could not spare their lorries; this 1915 Fiat 18BL was one of many similar types that remained on the Home Front. *Below centre* Even a 1-ton Studebaker found itself involved in hostilities. Its headlamps were masked so as to make it less of an obvious target. *Bottom* Many vehicles were adapted for military use including this Swiss Saurer 5-tonner.

commercial vehicle industry. The British government offered the purchaser of an approved vehicle a subsidy. However, the vehicle had to be handed over to the authorities within 72 hours of mobilization.

One of the most advanced British "subsidy" types was the 3½-ton Dennis 'A'-Type, although the 'L' or 'RAF'-Type Leyland was certainly the best known. The Dennis had considerable influence on British truck design after the war, its most striking feature being a rear axle with removable upper casing containing the worm shaft, worm wheel, differential and bearings, thus enabling the entire final-drive mechanism to be inspected or replaced without disturbing either the chassis or the wheels. Leyland Motors, on the other hand, built both a 1½-tonner and the 3-ton 'RAF'-Type, while Albion supplied 6000 "subsidy" vehicles, and the Associated Equipment Co Ltd over 10,000. Many of their London General Omni-

bus Co 'B'-Type open-top double-deck buses were also commandeered and ordered to the Front. The standardization of models and components required by the British "subsidy" scheme enabled so-called cannibalization to take place to keep transport moving, whereas the adoption of any suitable vehicle by the French and German forces gave no such advantage.

As the war progressed, so British forces began to take delivery of new American-built trucks designed specifically for arduous work. Amongst these was the Mack 'AC', nicknamed the "Bulldog" because of its snub nose and rugged construction. Ultimately, this became so well-known by its nickname that the bulldog was adopted as the Mack logo, which it remains to this day. Some American manufacturers, such as General Motors, were now concentrating almost exclusively on the construction of military vehicles, while certain European manufacturers,

Below In 1915 a new series of Internationals were launched. These introduced the 'coal-scuttle' bonnet to the US market. The radiator was carried behind the engine. *Below centre* Large numbers of US-built Peerless 5-tonners were also shipped to Europe. *Bottom left* With increasing competition between manufacturers, publicity stunts such as the GMC milk run from Seattle to New York, became all the rage. *Bottom right* This 1-ton 4x4 built in 1917 by the Wisconsin Duplex Auto Co was the ancestor of the modern Oshkosh range.

Left The Mack 'Bulldog', which was a chain-drive model, saw war service in Europe. Its name was apparently coined by British troops who thought that the pugnacious styling of the steel hood resembled a bulldog. The bulldog was quickly adopted as the company symbol. *Below* This early drawbar model of the 'Bulldog' series was produced in America. Even today examples of it can be found in various parts of the world.

such as MAN, Magirus in Germany or Société d'Outillage Mécanique et d'Usinage d'Artilleries (Somua) in France, were building their first trucks in an attempt to turn the tide. Indeed, Somua was established for the sole purpose of building army trucks.

Throughout the Western world, factories not involved in the manufacture of military trucks were turned over to the production of armaments such as shells, firearms and aero engines, while others manufactured both military vehicles and also armaments.

Many American-built trucks saw service not only in Europe but also in the Mexican border campaign of 1916, when the United States government waged war against the Mexican bandit Pancho Villa. This served as a proving ground for these trucks, many of which were later shipped to Europe for military service. At this time, few US-built military trucks were standardized, and it was not until the development of the US Quartermaster Corps's 'B'-Class heavy truck, known as the "Liberty", that proper standardization occurred.

On the civilian front, producer-gas was used to combat the lack of petrol, and in the United States the 1916 Federal Aid Road Act was instrumental in establishing a new interstate highway system which contributed greatly to the development of American commercial vehicles. With a rubber tyre shortage, particularly in Germany where manufacturers had relied upon British- and French-made supplies, unconventional steel-wheeled vehicles, sometimes incorporating metal plates backed by small leaf springs, appeared for a short while, but these were mainly for heavy tractors used for hauling artillery. Developments in commercial vehicle design, such as the use of shaft-drive, glass windscreens and electric rather than acetylene lighting, were now creeping in from the passenger car side and, although apparent in many light commercials, it was some years before these were adopted for the heavy commercial market. Pneumatic tyres were also becoming commonplace on lighter types but, again, were to remain a rarity on "heavies" for some time.

While the war did much to establish new standards for commercial vehicles, military vehicle requirements were far different from those used on the public highway. High payloads and economy were more important to civilian operators than high ground clearance or all-wheel drive. Thus, with a return to peace, much re-organization was necessary.

Peacetime development

WHILE the end of the war in 1918 opened the field to new manufacturers, it also presented new problems to the existing commercial motor industry. Some German armament producers, such as Krupp, were not allowed to continue production, and had to turn to the manufacture of trucks instead. However, vast quantities of ex-military vehicles were already being released into the civilian market and snapped up by both operators and thousands of servicemen anxious to set up in the expanding goods and passenger haulage business. In France alone there were thousands of American, British and German trucks scattered around, and although there were only some 400 licensed road hauliers in the United Kingdom at this time, by 1923 these had expanded to 2400, many of the vehicles being shipped into the country through ex-army dealers. Thus, demand for new vehicles was relatively low and sales suffered badly. Some manufacturers, such as Leyland Motors, established a re-conditioning plant for ex-WD trucks, while some dealers concentrated on particular makes such as the American Peerless and FWD, ultimately constructing vehicles of similar design and using the same identity.

By this time production equipment was out-of-date, and existing manufacturers were often faced with considerable re-tooling before new models could be introduced. Most, however, continued to concentrate on existing designs until 1923, due to a considerable slump in trade whereby those manufacturers which also built passenger cars found themselves with quantities of unsold cars. Another result of war-surplus trucks flooding the market was the effect on the road-going steamer, which was pushed further into the background by legislation and, ultimately, by the development of the diesel engine.

By 1919 the American, Malcolm Loughhead, had developed the 4-wheel Lockheed hydraulic braking system, and both Dunlop and Goodyear had announced their first pneumatic tyres. There was also increasing interest in large-capacity passenger vehicles.

Left Special facilities, such as the roof-mounted sleeper compartment on this 3-ton White, were needed for long-distance hauls in the USA. *Centre and bottom left* Specialist British municipal vehicles were led by the 3-wheeled Lacre roadsweeper; the French market was led by the DeDion 4-wheeler. *Right* Steam was still popular and even Leyland Motors offered an ''undertype'' wagon until 1926. *Bottom right* Vast numbers of ex-military trucks were now rapidly replacing the horse, particularly for transporting fuel.

Such change in social conditions resulted in the gradual development of vehicles built specifically to carry passengers. Some manufacturers which had been less fortunate during the war and had concentrated on the manufacture of armaments, were forced to start again with a small selection of lightweight commercials for passengers or payloads of up to 2½ tons. Existing passenger models, such as the 34-seat AEC 'B'-Type, were replaced by designs of even greater capacity, in this instance by the 46-seat 'K'-Type, and soon after by the 54-seat 'S'-Type. By 1923 the first of the famous 'NS'-Type, with its futuristic low-loading entrance, had appeared.

By the mid-1920s, road transport was becoming established and new ideas were plentiful. Forward-control or cab-over-engine layout were popular ways of increasing the load-carrying space, and Scammell Lorries Ltd, founded in 1921, built a 7½-ton 6-wheeled articulated lorry designed by Lt Col A G Scammell, DSO, which quickly led to other vehicles of similar layout. By 1925 a new 5/6-ton Dennis load-carrier had become the first Dennis to be powered by a monobloc engine with four integrally-cast cylinders and two detachable heads. The earlier charabanc was now being replaced by the sedate motor coach, one excellent example being the Albion 'Viking' of 1923. In 1924, Thornycroft built its first unit-construction vehicle, the A1 1½-tonner with engine, clutch and gearbox mounted as one unit at three points in the chassis frame. The old leather-to-metal clutch was now replaced by a single-plate unit and pneumatic tyres fitted. Pneumatics had been regarded with some scepticism by the authorities, as had 4-wheel brakes which were not permitted in London until 1926, when a suitably equipped Dennis 'E'-Type was tested on a hard surface with a coating of soft soap.

As a contrast to the European manufacturer, where each marque had an individual identity, and many parts were manufactured by the one company, the majority of American companies built vehicles which were purely assembled, using components which were available to anybody. It was not until the 1930s that this pattern began to change.

The rigid multi-wheeler

THE DEVELOPMENT of pneumatic tyres led to the construction of the first multi-wheeled goods and passenger models. Among the first rigid 6-wheelers were single- and double-drive conversions of the US Army's "Liberty" truck, followed by a new double-drive 4-wheel braked bogie developed by Hendrickson Mfg, of America, in 1924. With larger payloads, pneumatic-tyred 4-wheelers suffered increasingly from punctures, leading to the idea that the load should be distributed over two rear axles, with manufacturers adopting different layouts and drive systems. It was also discovered that 2-axle pneumatic-tyred bogies caused less damage to road surfaces than those of single-axle design.

Varying drive layouts were adopted for such bogies. The German Büssing organization drove each rear axle separately from an auxiliary gearbox located behind the main box, while the Scottish-built Caledon 6-wheeler had one "live" axle driving two "dead" ones by roller chain. Karrier was another British marque that was early on the 6-wheeled scene, using two under-worm axles. Guy Motors delivered the world's first 6-wheeled trolleybus to the Wolverhampton Corp in 1926, fitting a double-deck body and regenerative control. This company also built the world's first double-deck motorbus, as well as a small fleet of 6-wheeled double-deckers in 1927.

Another notable 6-wheeler was the Thornycroft A3, developed from the A1 "subsidy" lorry of 1924 and intended for cross-country operation. This was actually a military vehicle, but quickly caught on overseas where its worm-drive axles and auxiliary transmission established it as a worthwhile machine for both on- and off-road work. In military guise, the A3 could handle 1½-ton loads and, for civilian work, loads of up to 2½ tons could be managed. Cross-country tracks could be fitted over the rear wheels as required.

Meanwhile, on the passenger vehicle front, the Associated Daimler Co, formed from a short-lived liaison between Associated Equipment Co Ltd and Daimler Co Ltd, developed the

RUGBY TRUCKS are Engineered by Experts to Cut Haulage Costs

RUGBY

Spedition - Möbeltransport - Lagerung - Verpackung
E. Winkler & Co.
Görlitz

R. KEETCH & SON

Above The bonneted 4-wheeled arrangement was still preferred in Europe as on this 1922 Austrian-built Steyr street-washer. *Top* Rugby Trucks catered for the smaller end of the light-weight truck market. *Centre* Articulation meant greater capacity, an ideal solution for household removals, this operator is using a Magiruz-hauled outfit. *Above right and right* Multi-wheeled rigids were gaining in popularity on both sides of the Atlantic, demonstrated here by a 1929 Scammell 'Rigid-6' and in 1924 by a Mack "Bulldog". *Far right* Breweries were among the last strongholds of steam, this 6-ton Foden was delivered to the Openshaw Brewery Ltd in 1928.

massive Model 802 or "London Six", using a double-reduction worm bogie similar to that used in a 10-ton goods model produced by Brozincevic & Co, Zürich. The "London Six" was a breakthrough in that engine vibration was minimized by mounting the 6-cyl sleeve-valve unit in a subframe which was supported in the main chassis frame by a series of cushion pads, with final-drive effected by a central underslung worm-gear for each wheel and each axle's own differential.

By this time, the bonneted layout was the most popular for both goods and passenger models, and while some truck manufacturers shifted their allegiance to passenger cars, so others switched from cars to trucks, or added trucks to their product lines. One such was Morris Cars Ltd, which set up Morris Commercial Cars Ltd in 1924 to build a new 1-tonner, adding 1½- and 2-ton double-drive 6-wheelers within three years.

Many countries, such as Japan and the Soviet Union, were new to commercial vehicle manufacture, but were quick to develop reliable new models, often based on existing British or American designs. Indeed, it was Britain and America which set the example to many other countries, particularly with operating commercials, for in Britain alone, between 1919 and 1929, the number of operational goods vehicles rose from 62,000 to 330,000, and in America these figures were even higher.

Six-cyl petrol engines were now making their mark, the first 6-cyl Leyland commercial being the 'Titan' double-decker announced in 1927. The 'Titan' was also one of the first lowbridge double-deckers, with a sunken gangway in each saloon and an overall height of less than 4m. One of the most talked-about exhibits in 1927 was the Thornycroft 'Lightning' motor coach with a new side-valve 6-cyl petrol engine producing 70bhp. Some argued it was well ahead of its time, having vacuum-assisted 4-wheel brakes, but it merely pointed the way for other manufacturers.

Advances in these fields precipitated other changes. At Tilling-Stevens, petrol-electric propulsion was replaced by petrol power, with the introduction of the lightweight 4-cyl 'Express' passenger model, and by 1926 the world's first frameless tank semi-trailer had been pioneered by Scammell Lorries Ltd, Watford, Herts. By the end of the 1920s, the military lorry was rapidly disappearing in passenger and goods haulage circles. In 1928 the first oil-engined truck to enter service in the United Kingdom was a Mercedes-Benz, and one year later the Kerr-Stuart, the first all-British diesel lorry, arrived. Also in 1929, two of the world's heaviest vehicles, 100-ton Scammells, were constructed for heavy haulage work.

The depression

THE 1930s dawned with the Depression hanging over the world. Its influence meant that manufacturers and operators were beginning to use the diesel engine for motor vehicles, because it was more economical.

Diesel engines had been fitted experimentally in certain commercials from the mid-1920s, one of the first British examples being fitted to a London bus in 1928, but it was on the Continent that such developments grew, with Berliet of France fitting its first diesel in 1930, Renault in 1931, and Fiat of Italy in 4- and 6-tonners in 1931. Leyland Motors was also experimenting with diesel, and the Tilling-Stevens Express bus was offered with a 4-cyl diesel engine, but the first complete diesel-engined bus built in the United Kingdom was a 1931 Crossley.

Many of these engines were constructed along similar lines, but there were exceptions. Klockner-Humboldt-Deutz was looking at air-cooled units, but these were not fitted in any quantity until 1940. In the United States, both Cummins and General Motors (GM) were experimenting, the former fitting its first diesel, the Model 'H', to a truck in 1932, while GM pondered on the development of a 2-stroke diesel which did not go into full production until 1937.

While it was apparent that the diesel engine was the answer to the economic problem, many operators were still prejudiced as it was largely an unknown quantity.

Although some American manufacturers were developing diesel engines, there were others concentrating on the development of more powerful petrol units, as the United States had a plentiful supply of cheap home-produced petrol. Thus, the petrol engine dominated the field in the United States until the 1960s, when increasing dependency upon imported fuels led to an increased use of automotive diesels. Similarly, Germany relied upon imported fuel, and Hitler was quick to realize the importance of developing the country's own fuel source. Thus, diesel came to the fore.

Generally, there were two types of diesel engine – direct and indirect injection – although most were of the in-

direct type, as this was quieter and more economical. The advent of the diesel engine brought new-found wealth to many established concerns.

Fodens Ltd, of Sandbank, Cheshire, also went through considerable re-organization at this time with E R Foden and his son leaving the company to set up the diesel vehicle manufacturer ERF Ltd in 1933. Meanwhile Fodens itself continued vehicle building, changing from steam to diesel propulsion. Dennis Bros Ltd, of Guildford, Surrey, moved into the diesel field in 1935, with a version of its Lancet II passenger model powered by a Dennis Big Four petrol engine or a Dennis-Lanova low-compression diesel. One of the earliest diesel engine builders in Britain was W H Dorman & Co Ltd, whose first design was a 4-cyl job developing 20bhp at 1000rpm. This company built

Above The early 1930s were a crucial time for the California-based Fageol Motors Co, despite the production of short bonneted trucks with a low centre of gravity. *Left* When this Type 85 Alfa-Romeo was built in 1934 even bonneted trucks were beginning to reflect more modern styling. *Bottom left* The first passenger vehicle to carry the Bedford name was the 14-seater WHB built in 1931. *Top right* The 2½-ton FN was built in Belgium, powered by a straight 8 petrol engine. *Above middle right* The spoked wheels on this 1932 Kenworth were unusual for a vehicle operating on the west side of the US at this time. *Above bottom right* The Sentinel was one of the most advanced steam vehicles and the most famous was the multi-wheeled 58 of 1934. *Right* 'Commercial Car Journal' was now the leading road transport publication in the USA.

both the Dorman-Ricardo high-speed airless injection type and the direct-injection type, but in recent years has concentrated on the manufacture of industrial diesels rather than those for automotive use. Another firm which is synonymous with the production of automotive diesels is F Perkins Ltd, Peterborough, which was founded in 1932 to produce the P6 diesel, again popular as a conversion.

However, it was not just diesel developments which accelerated during the 1930s, as commercial bodywork was improving rapidly, particularly on the passenger vehicle side. Motor coach bodies throughout Europe and America were following passenger car styling, particularly in Germany, and ventilation and other comforts were much improved. Many coaches had sunshine roofs which could be folded back for all-weather

Right The Latil 'Traulier' was a French design combining the manouevrability of 4-wheel steering with the go-anywhere characteristics of 4-wheel drive. *Below right* Morris-Commercial's 3-ton C9/60, although of bonneted layout, had its engine protruding into the cab giving it a "snub-nosed" appearance. *Below* Legislation was now forcing breweries to change from steam to diesel, by going with this trend manufacturers such as Foden (whose logo appears below) managed to retain their customers.

operation, and both buses and coaches were far more comfortable.

By the mid-1930s, with the exception of trolleybuses, 6-wheeled passenger models were vanishing while 4-axle rigid goods models were offered by most British diesel-engined goods vehicle manufacturers. The use of articulated load-carriers was catching on, and in the United States, the first "double bottoms" – articulated vehi-

cles with an extra drawbar trailer – were beginning to appear on the longer inter-state routes. In urban areas, there was the "mechanical horse", a strange 3-wheeled tractor replacing the horse and cart, built mainly in Britain by Scammell and Karrier. This vehicle was specially devised to hitch up to horse-drawn carts, particularly used by railway companies to speed deliveries. A derivative of

this was the 3-wheeled Ford Tug of 1935, which had a Model 'Y' van body.

A bonneted layout was still the norm for heavy commercials but forward-control was becoming increasingly popular, due to the fact that more load-carrying space was now available.

However, a generally conservative attitude ensured that the bonnet-

Top left German manufacturers were now well ahead, both in vehicle design and in the development of new propulsion systems. This Magirus-Deutz had an underfloor engine running on producer gas. *Middle left above* The Czechoslovakian Tatra T82 6-wheeler of 1936 had an air-cooled diesel engine. *Above* Aerodynamic styling became the vogue in North America and Canada at this time. Labart's Canadian brewery took delivery of this spectacular White in 1937. *Left* The ERF C1561 6-wheeler had a 5-cylinder Gardner diesel engine and was popular with many British hauliers during the 1930s and 1940s.

ed arrangement would continue for some time. As the distance between delivery points increased, so the use of sleeper cabs grew, mainly on the Continent and in the United States, and to make the driver's job even easier, power-steering began to appear. Suspensions were improved, some incorporating rubber units, and brake systems were up-dated to make the heavier trucks, buses and coaches safer.

Hydraulic braking was offered on many 4-wheeled rigids, although multi-wheeled rigids and artics were still without brakes on some axles. In Switzerland, Italy and France, the first exhaust brakes, suited to mountainous terrains, began to appear, and in America particularly, automatic or semi-automatic transmissions were being fitted.

In common with passenger body-

work, truck bodies were beginning to be constructed of light-alloy, and some American manufacturers were even building truck and van bodies on line-flow principles. Also in America, increasing use was being made of lightweight materials, even in chassis manufacture, and by the end of the 1930s most of the present-day leading truck and bus manufacturers were in business.

World war II

THROUGHOUT the latter half of the 1930s, the world was relentlessly moving towards another war. The German Schell Programme of 1938 called for the standardization of military truck production, segregating vehicles into light-, medium- and heavy-duty types from 1 to 6½ tons payload with engines of a given minimum output. These ideas were later reflected in the commercial truck boom of the 1950s and 1960s when German-built trucks had to have a minimum of 8bhp per ton of a vehicle's gross weight.

By 1939 the German forces were prepared for hostilities. While many hard lessons had been learned during World War I, some countries were still lagging behind in vehicle production. In Britain, production of military vehicles and equipment was stepped up towards the end of the 1930s, although many military trucks were merely militarized versions of commercial models. The larger manufacturers, such as Leyland Motors, moved into armaments production, while others, such as Austin and Morris-Commercial, concentrated on trucks and artillery tractors.

Weight did not matter as much as the vehicle's ability to go anywhere, and sturdily constructed 4 x 4, 6 x 4 and 6 x 6 trucks were rushed off the production lines. One British manufacturer which was prepared was Guy Motors, Wolverhampton, which had abandoned civilian in favour of government contracts in the mid-1930s, concentrating on production of the 4-wheel drive 'Quad-Ant', an 8 x 8 load-carrier, and, after 1941, a civilian version of the 'Quad-Ant' known as the 'Vixen'. The best known 3-ton army trucks were to be the Bedford QL 4 x 4 and 'OY'-Series 4 x 2, of which, at the time, nearly 1000 a week were being built. Both Commer and Karrier also built 4 x 4s, but perhaps the most well remembered of the period were the 4 x 4 AEC Matador medium artillery tractor and the massive Scammell Pioneer range of artillery, tank recovery and vehicle breakdown models based on Scammell Lorries' pre-war oilfield and heavy haulage tractor.

Although British and American forces moved their tanks by road on

Above The Morris-Commercial C8 was one of the most profilic field artillery tractors on the Allied side.
Left German Forces were great users of the hybrid half-truck. This was the 2-ton Magirus-Deutz 53000/SSM.
Left bottom: A 1943 Bedford QL, which was one of the most familiar 3-ton 4 x 4's in the British Services.

The Marines Grab a Foothold!

Just a foothold—that's all they ask. Tropic mud or arctic snow—they are all the same to the Marines.

Like the Marines, the motorized equipment used by them usually has a strictly "off-the-highway" job. A typical unit is this rugged, 2½-ton truck, fittingly named the "Marine 6 by 6." It is noteworthy for its lower silhouette, its husky power plant and, above all, for its tremendous tractive ability.

THORNTON
Automatic-Locking
DIFFERENTIAL

in both rear driving axles eliminates wheel-spin and gives positive traction in mud, sand, snow or ice.

These THORNTON qualities that serve the Marines so well . . . sturdiness, tractive ability, dependability . . . fit equally well into other military vehicles.

The THORNTON
full driving torque to e
or mud.

Thus there is no u
under conditions wh

THORNTON TA
8711-8779 GRINNELL AVE.
Manufacturers also of the THORNTON Fou
"When you need TRACTION you

Top and extreme right Two US truck advertisements. The competitive nature of many US truck advertisements turned to propaganda at the end of the 1930s as World War II got under way. *Right* Diamond T production lines, showing part of the "Six-by-Six" and "Tank-hauler" production. Diamond T's war truck production exceeds the normal peacetime heavy-truck output of the entire automotive industry.

Another Fleet of Locomotive-Sized Federals
GOES ON THE WAR PATH TO VICTORY

★ The operation pictured above is somewhere in the Canadian Northwest, where airfields, coast artillery, gun emplacements and military roads have become vital in the defense of America. These works—now completed —or being rushed to completion—are important to our protective strategy. They serve to illustrate how hundreds of fleets of husky Federal Trucks have been doing legion work, aiding in the all important job of protecting the Arsenals of Democracy from land, air or sea invasion— hastening the day of Victory.

Many months before Pearl Harbor, Federal Trucks were in wide use with our own and the United Nations' Armed Forces. Today Federal Trucks are operating in the combat and defensive areas of the Middle East, Alaska, the Canal Zone, India, Russia, China, Britain, Canada, Australia and the U. S. A.

Hundreds of uses, in thousands of jobs, as armored tank haulers, giant aircraft rescue trucks, road builders, airfield construction units, fire fighters and heavy transport carriers, are proving over and over again how Federal's "all-truck", balanced design is recognized for long-lived dependability and consistent, top flight performance. That's why those in important positions on both our work fronts and war fronts demand Federal's huskier, heavy duty reliability. They're tossing the tough jobs to Federal because they know they'll deliver!

FEDERAL MOTOR TRUCK COMPANY, DETROIT, MICHIGAN

The Army and Navy "E" was awarded to Federal—"For Excellence in War Production"—building thousands of heavy duty trucks for our Armed Forces.

FEDERAL TRUCKS
Since 1910 . . . Known in Every Country—Sold on Every Continent

Top right The austere Fiat 626N 3-tonner of 1939 was used by civilians as well as by the Armed Forces. *Far right middle* The Model 1506 cab fitted to civvy GMC's in 1941 was plain to say the least. *Extreme far right middle* Due to the vast numbers of vehicles needed, many US manufacturers built vehicles of standard design. This Mormon-Herrington H-542-11 5-ton tractor was based on International Harvester designs. *Far bottom right* This AEC 'Mammoth Major III' was supplied in 1941 for essential civilian use. *Right* An Austin K4 (16) which was used in peacetime as a coal truck.

transporters, thereby causing them much wear and tear, the Germans preferred to use rail. The Allies also perfected the movement of other heavy loads and, with a return to peace, adapted these methods to the haulage and construction industries, often using ex-military equipment. Articulation was used, particularly for hauling aircraft components such as wings and fuselages, and Scammell Lorries again came to the fore in the supply of general cargo or tank semi-trailers with automatic couplings.

One American-built truck worthy of special mention was the 6 x 6 GMC of which more than 600,000 were built. This became a real army work-horse and was adopted for a surprising number of tasks. There were many much heavier types as well, such as those produced by Autocar, Diamond T, Kenworth, Oshkosh, Reo and White, as well as numerous lighter types.

Although much of the world's truck production was given over to military types, civilian models were still being built. In France, for example, Berliet was producing wood-burning trucks which ran on the gas resulting from the combustion process but this ended with the Occupation, when manufacturers were forced to supply vehicles to the German forces. However, it was the French heavy vehicle industry that was hardest hit by World War II, although Allied bombers also left little of the German truck plants standing.

By 1941 fuel shortages were a serious problem throughout Europe. Even bus operators could not obtain sufficient supplies, and many of these vehicles were withdrawn, while others were converted to operate with producer-gas trailers. Some single-deckers even ran on town gas stored in huge tent-like structures mounted on the roof. A year later certain manufacturers, such as Guy Motors, were authorized to build austerity versions of their passenger models to replace pre-war vehicles wrecked or damaged. To clear bomb damage or haul heavy machinery, traction engines and other extinct types were moved into service.

Off road & construction vehicles

Following World War I many hundreds of all-wheel drive and other heavy specification military trucks came onto the civilian market and were quickly snapped up by the construction industry and others requiring heavy-duty vehicles. New civilian versions were soon developed for on/off-road working and even larger strictly off-road types gradually developed, principally for mining and quarrying. The most common off-road types are now dump trucks. There are other designs which have been developed specifically for the building and construction industries; these include drilling rigs, lorry-mounted cranes and concrete mixers.

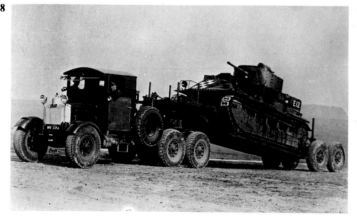

1 The twin-engined rotary snowplough built around 1920 by the Winther Motor Truck Co, Wisconsin was unusual for its day. 2 A 1919 Walker Model 'K' 1-ton battery-electric integral van. 3 The front-discharge unit is an increasingly popular feature. In the case of the 'B'-Series Oshkosh it incorporated a rear-mounted engine, a centrally placed one-man cab and a 6x6 layout. 4 Off-highway dump trucks such as this rear-wheel drive Terex 33-11B are the real construction giants. 5 This 6x6 Autocar construction truck, made by the White Motor Corp. can cope with very heavy work. 6/7 The 'Lowline' crane carrier is of almost universal appeal, it is exemplified here by the Mitsubishi Fuso K600 60-tonner.

8/9 An early prototype Scammell 'Pioneer' equipped with all-over tracks shows off its capabilities while Scammell's first tank transporter recovers a disabled truck. 10 The British-built AIM 'Stalwart' 6x6 with full independent suspension and steering on all but the last two wheels was adopted by the military authorities of many countries as a standard amphibious land-carrier. 11 The US-built NOZ Mack of the 1940s was a 7½-ton 6x6 with double-reduction gearing in the steering ends of the front axle which provided a higher front axle than the vehicle's hubs.

The post-war years

THE WESTERN WORLD of 1945 was far different from that of 1919. Not only was there a shortage of materials (the most important being steel), but also monetary restrictions out-of-date equipment, and a lack of skilled labour. In the United Kingdom, the government decided to increase exports, and insisted that sixty percent of total vehicle exports should comprise commercial vehicles. By 1946 the government's seemingly impossible sales figures had been reached, simply by selling more vehicles abroad than before the war.

British manufacturers continued mainly with pre-war ranges, such as the bonneted Commer 'Superpoise', launched in 1939, and the Bedford 'O'-Type, also a normal-control design. This gave firms sufficient breathing space to introduce totally new models like the forward-control underfloor-engined Commer of 1948, and the 'Big Bedford' of 1950. This had a 4.9-litre 6-cyl petrol engine, regarded by many as the best petrol engine ever fitted in a commercial.

The 1947 British Transport Act led to the nationalization of road haulage, which in turn resulted in fleet standardization and other improvements. By 1948, United Kingdom commercial vehicle exports were five times higher than in 1938, and British expertise led

the world. Leyland engines and other components were used in the first DAF trucks and many United Kingdom manufacturers, particularly the premium truck and bus builders like Fodens, Atkinson, ERF and Leyland, concentrated on Commonwealth markets, such as Northern and Southern Rhodesia, South Africa and Australia. Mergers became commonplace in an effort to consolidate activities, with AEC acquiring Crossley in 1948 and Maudslay in 1949, while Leyland bought Albion in 1951, and Scammell in 1955.

The Japanese now have one of the world's largest vehicle industries, certainly as far as exports are concerned, but in 1946 it was still in its infancy. Hino's first truck was a 15-ton capacity artic announced in 1946, followed one year later by an air-braked articulated bus. Volume production did not get underway until 1949, the company's heaviest model being a 6 x 6 10-tonner introduced in 1951. During these early days of the Japanese motor industry there were close ties with European manufacturers such as Renault and Rootes, but once established in their own right, these ties were quickly broken.

The immediate post-war period was the heyday of the American truck-building industry, with products being

Far left and top left For countries that had been involved in the war, many post-war models were the same as pre-war types. Both the Foden DG6/15 and the Belford 'M'-type fall into this category. *Bottom left* After the war Leyland developed a number of all-steel cabs with forward-control such as this 'Beaver'. *Above* The 'KB'-Line International of 1947 was a much modified and improved version of the pre-war 'K'-Series. *Right* In 1950 GMC announced a new "weight-saving" diesel tractor which used much more light alloy than before.

GMC
TRUCKS

Far right The WF800 Freightliner "cabover", designed by a truck operator became the White Freightliner when White took over Freightliner sales and service in 1951. Meanwhile, the White Motor Co's own idea of a medium-weight "cabover" was the tiltcab '3000' series. *Right and below* Peterbilt and Kenworth were custom-building their heavy-duty "conventionals".

sold worldwide. It was at this time that American manufacturers set the trend for heavy "cabover" articulated tractor units for long-distance haulage, employing many ideas gleaned from the war years and, in particular, from aircraft production. Aluminium alloy was being used in increasing quantities, not only for components but also for body sections and framing. Some of the larger manufacturers were even acquiring individual body-building concerns, so that vehicle bodies, such as light- and mediumweight panel vans, could be produced by that manufacturer.

Since World War II there have been two major innovations in the commercial vehicle field. One is the almost universal adoption of articulation, and the other the use of forward-control tilt-cabs. Articulation has now developed furthest in the United States where, since the 1950s, "double-bottom" outfits comprising one tractor, a dolly and two semi-trailers, have become common. In Europe a drawbar configuration is still the most popular, whilst articulation rates as the most popular method in the United Kingdom.

The use of forward-control tilt-cabs in the United States only really caught on in the 1950s, before which time bonneted tractors were more popular. However, the "cabover" layout permits longer semi-trailers to be used, thereby making vehicle operations more economical.

New technology

WITH A WORLDWIDE INCREASE in prosperity, the accent was placed on vehicle design, although great advances were still being made in other aspects of vehicle manufacture, particularly their efficiency. At the 1948 Commercial Motor Show, Fodens Ltd exhibited a new 4-cyl 2-stroke diesel engine which was to herald a new technological age for the commercial vehicle. It was a particularly efficient design, followed in 1955 by a 3-cyl Rootes 2-stroke for diesel or multi-fuel applications. Turbocharged diesels were first used in trucks by Volvo of Sweden, where gross weights are

Far right top A 1953 Volvo L375 4/5 ton truck. *Middle top* In spite of being functional, the bonneted French Willème was a decidedly ugly vehicle. *Right top* Built in France in 1955 this Latil was unlikely to be seen outside France. *Right* The 1956 bonneted Bedford was a very versatile truck that did much to boost Britain's export figures. *Below* This crew-cabbed petrol-engined Dennis was typical of the vehicles operated by many British local authorities at the time.

the highest in Europe. Instead of building larger engines to produce greater power, Volvo fitted a turbo compressor which enabled as much as fifty percent more power to be produced by each engine. This system was announced in 1954 and, as well as giving increased power output, offers low fuel consumption and quiet running.

Petrol engines were still popular in the United States after World War II, but as the 1950s progressed, the use of diesels in heavy trucks became the norm. Mack Trucks announced its 'Thermodyne' diesel in 1953, and by the early 1960s many British-built Perkins diesels were being fitted in even light- and mediumweight delivery models, and high-speed 'V'-form diesels were being used both in the United States and Europe. Agreements were signed between the American-owned Cummins Engine Co, Jaguar in the United Kingdom, and Krupp in Germany, to manufacture Cummins engines in Europe under the Jaguar-Cummins and Krupp-Cummins brand names. These agreements, however, were later cancelled and Cummins 'V' engines built in quantity in the company's British plant. While some, such as Cummins and Scania, have developed successful 'V' diesels, others have not. AEC, Southall, Middx, developed its own V8 unit, known as the '800'-Series, but this was unsuccessful.

The new era

During the 1960s there was considerable interest in the use of gas-turbine power for both trucks and buses, and a number of prototypes were built. Many of the leading American manufacturers investigated this source of power and in the United Kingdom, British Leyland developed four vehicles. However, with the exception of the massive Lectra-Haul dump truck, which is powered by an 1100bhp Saturn gas-turbine, none of these reached production stage and the cost of fuel is now prohibitive.

Recent years have seen the opening up of large areas of the world to long-distance trucking largely due to the construction of motorways and other major routes. The Asian Highway was just one example, having a considerable effect on European road haulage and, eventually, on the design of vehicles operating over long distances. Many manufacturers began offering a special "Middle East" package on heavier trucks and tractor units, with features which provided maximum driver comfort. Vehicle braking systems and tyres have improved as distances and speeds have increased, so that the modern long-haul artic unit invariably relies upon full air brakes, while intermediate types have adopted air/hydraulic systems. More recently, exhaust brakes and other forms of engine retarder have appeared more frequently.

Left Scammell's 'Highwayman' was particularly popular as an artic tanker, special versions of it were frequently sold abroad. This one was sold to Venezuela. *Bottom far left* The Mercedes-Benz artic truck was popular in the UK in the 60s.

It was a bonneted model and had forward-control. *Bottom centre* A mini revolution in the UK cab design resulted in some very pleasing models. ERF's 'LV' cab was a case in point. *Bottom right* This mass-produced Ford Thames 'Trader' was now a familiar sight on British roads.

Truck transmissions have also changed. It is only since the war that synchromesh transmissions have appeared in large numbers, and by the early 1960s range-change transmissions and 2-speed axles were increasingly popular. Automatic or semi-automatic transmissions also have their place, but have never gained much popularity in the truck field. On the suspension front, air systems have become commonplace on passenger models but are still comparatively rare on trucks, being more popular for vehicles carrying bulk liquids than on those for general goods.

A further revolution in road transport has been created by the movement of containers on an international scale and the use of special pallets to aid mechanical handling. As recently as the 1960s, truck drivers had to load, sheet and rope their own vehicles, and some still do, but in the main the loads are now containerized or palletized, simplifying the operation considerably. In some countries, such as France, even the semi-trailers are specially built to be carried on "Kangaroo" rail wagons, thereby eliminating long trips by road, but in the main, containers of standard dimensions are used internationally, enabling complete interchangeability.

Left British trucks for the Australian market were very different from their UK counterparts, roadtrains such as this AEC 'Mammoth Major' hauled outfit being commonplace in the outback. *Centre left* Concentrating on custom-built trucks, the Hendrickson Mfg. Co. Illinois, offered its Model 'B' tipper to virtually any specification. *Centre right* At the heavier end of the UK market was the Thorneycroft 'Antor' C6T. It sold to military and heavy haulage customers, this example being exported to Argentina. *Bottom left* By the end of the decade AB Volvo was expanding rapidly in export fields. Despite the dated appearance of this bonnetted range it was well suited for this market. *Bottom centre* The Hino 'T.E.' – F series tipper of 1966 was another very straightforward design. *Bottom right* American regulations permit the use of double and triple-bottom long-haul outfits such as this GMC 'Astro' machine.

The present and the future

THE 1970s could be truly termed the technological age as far as the commercial vehicle is concerned. We have already seen how the gas-turbine was seriously considered at the end of the previous decade as an alternative to petrol or diesel power for the heavier vehicle and how this possibility was brought to an abrupt halt by the fuel crisis. Meanwhile, in a further attempt to produce an economical substitute fuel for use in road vehicles, experiments got under way in most countries into the feasibility of battery-electric propulsion, the major obstacle being that of weight. Leaders in this field are General Motors in the USA and the Lucas-Chloride partnership in the UK, although a recent announcement from British Rail's Technical Centre in Derby suggests that they may at last have developed a lightweight sodium-sulphur battery suitable for road use.

The last decade has also seen increasing interest in the protection of the environment which has frequently backfired on the road transport operator in the form of lorry cordons and other restrictive legislation. From the bureaucratic angle, the EEC (Common Market) has also had much effect throughout Europe, making the tachograph ('spy in the cab') compulsory in member countries and reducing permissible driving hours. Connected both with this and the environmentalists' attitude, there have also been attempts, largely unsuccessful, to transfer goods from road to rail. Certain European countries no longer permit heavy trucks to operate on Sundays, substituting instead a railway service on which all lorries are carried.

In many countries the weights and size of vehicles has gradually increased and in Britain experiments are being conducted with American-style double-bottom outfits, comprising tractor, semi-trailer, drawbar dolly and second semi-trailer, for motorway operation. Abnormal and indivisible loads have also become heavier, with some European specialists now offering a transport service for individual loads in excess of 500 tons.

There have been even more changes in the manufacturing side of

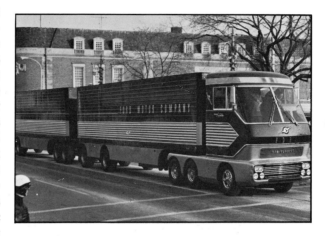

Above left By the early 1970s "Big Red", Ford of America's gas-turbine prototype, was becoming a thing of the past rather than the future. *Above* The EEC introduced UK truckers to tachographs. These record drivers' hours and the vehicle operations. They were phased in gradually towards the end of the 70s. *Left* MAN's giant X-90 project with roof-mounted sleeping compartments looks to the future. *Below* The oil crisis of the mid-1970s inspired this prototype of a wedge-shaped Paymaster. It was designed by an Oregon trucker. *Right* Chevrolet's 'Turbo Titan III', a gas-turbine powered aerodynamically styled vehicle whose low silhouette provided low wind resistance.

the business, with some old-established concerns taken over and sometimes even closed down completely. A classic example is that of British Leyland which had already acquired the manufacturing plants for AEC, Albion, Bristol, Guy, Scammell and Thornycroft, discontinuing all except Bristol and Scammell, by the end of the 1970s. In America, meanwhile, Daimler-Benz AG of Germany has acquired the Freightliner Corp' and, subject to confirmation, AB Volvo of Sweden has purchased the huge White Motor Corp, taking over assembly of

Top **The cab on the Berlet-derived TR305 is also used by Ford on its 'Transcontinental' model.** *Above* **As continental manufacturers moved in on the British market so new models gradually emerged to please UK operators. A DAF offering is the rigid-8 2300.** *Right* **Volvos have been built to survive the arduous weather conditions of Scandinavia, so it is not surprising that the heavier models with their rugged specifications have carved a niche for themselves in long-haul transport operations in other parts of the world. European operators using the F88 and F89 ranges led the field in the race to North Africa, the Middle East, and beyond in the mid-1970s.**

Custom rigs

Originating mainly in the United States, the custom rig is gradually spreading throughout the Western World, particularly among owner drivers. Special paint jobs and the fitting of chromed accessories are essential to the custom rig operator who, through these means, is able to express his individuality. There is now such a demand for this that virtually all US truck manufacturers now offer special paint schemes, following the lead set by companies such as Freightliner, Kenworth, Mack and Peterbilt, many of whose sales are aimed at the owner driver. Custom paint shops now also cater for trucks.

Top An imaginative 'cowboy' image is carried by this White Western Star. *Above* These two White Western Star tractors show just how far some manufacturers are prepared to go. *Far left* This fancy Kenworth "conventional" is definitely not ex-factory. *Left* These Kenworth paint jobs were specially developed for the owner-operator.

White, Autocar and Western Star trucks. These moves have been brought about by the search for still wider markets by European manufacturers.

Passenger transportation has also altered in the last decade, particularly in Britain. By the end of the 1960s the familiar half-cab double-decker which had been the mainstay of British bus operations for many years, was no longer in production, being superseded by mainly rear-engined full-front models easily adapted for one-man operation. As in the truck business, Britain's bus fleets were gradually infiltrated by similar vehicles of Continental origin, notably the Metro-Scania and Volvo 'Ailsa'.

For many years the articulated single-decker for fast urban operation had been popular in Europe and Scandinavia, especially in Germany and Sweden, and as in the case of the double-bottom goods vehicle, the British authorities permitted experiments with these on public roads. Similar arrangements were made in the USA, again using imported European models, and the idea is now being adopted almost worldwide with MAN, Scania and Volvo in the forefront.

In common with most other manufacturing industries, the world's commercial vehicle industry has suffered badly from the economic recession of the last few years. Some new marques, such as Ginaf, Stonefield, Terberg and Titan, have appeared during this time but even some of these have experienced financial problems. There is little doubt that the recession will have a continuing effect upon both commercial vehicle manufacturing and operating and some will find their only course is to close down. While this situation prevails, significant developments are likely to be few unless in the cause of economy. In the face of the gradual erosion of the world's oil resources, the search for new fuels will certainly continue, but there remains much development work to be done in this field.

The quest for fuel economy and more power has seen various developments in the engine field. In the USA, where petrol-engined trucks were the norm at the end of the 1960s, the diesel now reigns supreme, the cost of petrol being largely prohibitive. American truck operations have also been affected by a blanket 55mph speed limit, again in the interests of economy. In Europe, meanwhile, the fixed-head diesel engine gained brief popularity as a maintenance-free unit, only to fall down on length of operational life, but turbocharging, largely pioneered by AB Volvo, is obviously here to stay. 'V'-configuration engines are particularly popular in Germany where Mercedes and Magirus are the leaders.

Top far left The Scottish-built Ailsa double-decker, with Volvo components, illustrated the British approach to urban transit operations. *Top centre left* The 'juggernaut' syndrome of the 1970s encouraged Mercedes to develop a less imposing heavy truck cab without sacrificing its capabilities. *Left* This early model of Leyland's 'Roadtrain' (built in 1980), the 16-28 incorporated many components that can be adapted for virtually any size or weight of vehicle. *Centre far left* The Maxeter 'Flexibus' which uses Mercedes running gears. *Centre left* For basic ruggedness Scammell's 'Crusader' became the general haulage vehicle of the early 1970s, often carrying a sleeper car which makes it suitable for long-distance work. *Bottom far left* The 1978 Fiat truck range illustrates the marque's design similarities which could lead to more economic production. *Bottom centre* West coast styling from General Motors in this GMC 'General'. *Below* Kenworth continued to build West coach types, both "cabovers" and "conventionals".

Golden oldies

Because of the numerous changes in truck and bus safety legislation over the years the 'oldie' in its original form is often unacceptable as a roadworthy vehicle. However, these vehicles can be adapted to meet new regulations and have often been successfully modified.

Vehicle recovery specialists and travelling showmen are among those who have appreciated the potential of the 'oldie', often through necessity rather than choice. They have converted ex-military and cheap commercially operated designs and adapted them, for their own use to today's standards. Through working and caring for their vehicle they will have found out a great deal about it.

1 After World War II the ex-Service AEC 'Matador' 0853 4x4 became one of the best known recovery vehicles in Europe. 2 A 1950 Freightliner (foreground) and a 1940 'E'-Series Mack (behind) still in use in 1963. 3 Even this semi forward-control Mack is now in the 'oldie' class.

5

6

7

4 A fleet of AEC's, some of them Maudslays in disguise used by fairground people in the early 1960's. 5 With its custom paint job this ex-Services Mack NOZ 6x6 carried a fairground organ inside its restored timber body. 6 In 1952 a typical East coast offering was the 'conventional' Diamond T, another type that outlived many of its competitors. 7 The Gardner-engined Foden 'DG' range, typified by this 1939 DG6/15, survived longer than most types.

Pioneers

AUSTIN, Herbert *(1866-1941)*
Herbert Austin was born at Little Missenden, Bucks, in November 1866 and by 1883 had emigrated to Australia where he became an engineering manager. In 1890 he returned to the British Isles and took up an appointment as Director of the Wolseley Sheep-Shearing Co, Birmingham, designing this company's first motorcar, a 3-wheeler, in 1895. The first 4-wheeler, also designed by Austin, appeared in 1900 and by 1906 he had set up his own production facility in the Longbridge Works, Birmingham, developing this into the huge Austin Motor Co Ltd.

Knighted in 1917 and a Conservative MP from 1919 until 1924, Austin became a baron in 1936. He died at Bromsgrove, Worcs, in May 1941.

Carl F. Benz

BENZ, Carl F *(1844-1929)*
Carl Friedrich Benz was born in 1844 at Karlsruhe, Germany, and his early career was as a mechanical engineer. In 1883 he founded Benz & Cie at Mannheim to build stationary internal combustion engines, designing and constructing the world's first practical internal combustion engined motor car which first ran early in 1885 and was patented in January 1886.

In 1893 Benz built his first 4-wheeled car and introduced the first of a series of racing cars in 1899. By 1906 he had left the firm to set up C Benz Söhne, Ladenburg, with sons Eugen and Richard. He died on 4 April 1929.

BOLLEE, Amédée père *(1844-1917)*
Amédée Bollée Snr, born in 1844, ran the family bell-founding business in Le Mans, France, but was inspired by certain steam-powered exhibits at the Paris World Exhibition in 1867 to construct a fast private carriage, establishing a motor vehicle workshop in a corner of the foundry. The machine was far in advance

Amédée Bollée Snr

of anything that had gone before, following its own design parameters rather than those of horse-drawn or rail-borne vehicles.

He next constructed two 4-wheel drive 4-wheel steer tramcars with independent suspension and followed these with a new steam carriage with engine ahead of the driver and boiler at the rear. This he exhibited at the 1878 Paris World Exhibition, setting up a new workshop outside the family bell foundry, but a royalty agreement with a German manufacturer was unsuccessful and the collapse of this business led to Bollée's gradual disinterest in vehicle-building. He reverted to bell-founding, passing all vehicle enquiries to his eldest son, also Amédée Bollée.

BOLLEE, Amédée *fils (1868-1926)*
Amédée Bollée Jnr was just 18 when his father passed a steam carriage order to him. He had already built a light 2-seater for himself but this new project was a 16-seat double mail coach for the Marquis de Brox. He was not very successful in the steam sphere but opted instead for the petrol-driven motor car, the first of which he constructed in 1896, his designs being built under licence by De Dietrich.

He regularly took part in speed trials and this experience taught him the importance of aerodynamics. He built a number of machines with unusual torpedo-shaped bodies which led to numerous orders. By 1900 he had withdrawn from speed events and was concentrating instead on the construction of refined limited-production vehicles.

BOLLEE, Leon *(1870-1913)*
Amédée Bollée Jnr's younger brother, Léon, concentrated on the development of automatic machinery until the age of 26, showing one of the earliest automatic calculating machines at the 1889 Paris Exhibition. However, 1896 saw a new 3-wheeled motorcar which was the first vehicle to

be sold with pneumatic tyres as standard. Examples were built in England as well as France but within three years a new Léon Bollée design was under construction in the Darracq factory.

From 1903 Léon started to manufacture his own vehicles, backed financially and thus securely by the Vanderbilt family. Although he died in 1913, the Léon Bollée range continued for some years.

CHRYSLER, Walter P *(1875-1940)*
Walter Percy Chrysler was born at Wamego, Kansas, in 1875 and was later apprenticed to the Union Pacific Railroad machine shop. Joining the American Locomotive Co, he worked up to the position of Plant Manager but seeing opportunities elsewhere became Works Manager at the Buick Motor Co for half the salary. By 1916 he was President, building the Buick operation into the strongest of all General Motors subsidiaries by the time he left in 1919.

Six months later he took over the helm of both the Willys-Overland Co and the Maxwell Motor Co. These formed the basis of the Chrysler Corp, founded in 1925, which quickly introduced his own design of high-compression engined car. This became so successful that Maxwell production was discontinued.

In 1928 Chrysler purchased the Dodge Bros Manufacturing Co from the bank that had controlled it since the Dodge brothers' deaths, enabling him to launch the Plymouth range in 1928 as a new competitor for both Ford and Chevrolet.

Amédée Bollée Jnr

CITROEN, Andre G *(1878-1935)*
André Gustave Citroën, born in Paris on 5 February 1878, was both an engineer and an industrialist who was strongly in favour of Henry Ford's mass-production techniques, himself boosting Mors car and commercial production from 125 to 1200 units per year. He even convinced the French

Army that mass-production of munitions was essential during World War I and he set up a factory to do just this, later converting the plant into an automotive works. Refusing to admit defeat during the Depression, he introduced the only popular front-wheel drive car of the day. The company was made bankrupt in 1934 and Citroën lost control, dying in July 1935.

DAIMLER, Gottlieb W *(1834-1900)*
Gottlieb Wilhelm Daimler was born at Schorndorf, Württemburg, in 1834, and like Carl Benz became a mechanical engineer and inventor. At 38 he joined Eugen Langen and Nikolaus Otto at the Deutz Works in Cologne to assist with the development of a 4-stroke petrol engine. He soon became a leading figure in automotive development, setting up a workshop at Canstatt with Wilhelm Maybach in 1882 and pat-

Léon Bollée

enting one of the world's first high-speed internal combustion engines in December 1883, following this with a new design of carburettor.

In 1885 Daimler developed one of the world's first motorcycles, a 4-wheeled self-propelled carriage in 1886, a boat in 1887 and a 4-wheeled motorcar in 1889. The French rights to his engine patents were sold to Panhard et Levassor and in 1890 he founded Daimler-Motoren-Gesellschaft, again at Canstatt, to produce more motor vehicles, one of which was the Mercedes car, named after Co-Director Émile Jellinek's daughter. Daimler died in Canstatt on 6 March 1900.

DURANT, William C *(1861-1947)*
William Crapo Durant was born at Boston, Massachusetts, on 8 December 1861, and by 1886 had set up a carriage-building business in Michigan. After taking over another firm he began to construct Buick cars, merging this

Walter P. Chrysler

operation with those of several other manufacturers to form the General Motors Co in 1908. Due to financial wheeler-dealing, he lost control in 1910 but established the Chevrolet Motor Co with ex-racing driver Louis Chevrolet.

By manipulating shares, Durant placed this operation in a position where it was able to take over the General Motors Co in 1915 to form the General Motors Corp, with Durant as President. Business expanded well but the post World War I sales slump forced him out again in 1920. Undeterred, he founded Durant Motors Inc, again taking over various smaller organizations to diversify operations but neither this nor later ventures were very successful. He died in New York City in 1947.

FODEN, Edwin R *(1870-1950)*
Edwin Richard Foden was born on 28 March 1870 and followed in his father's footsteps with a great interest in things mechanical. His father ran the Foden traction engine and threshing machine business in Sandbach, Cheshire, and young Edwin was soon advising him on points of design. One of these was to construct a 2-cylinder machine that was both easier to start and smoother-running, thus leading to many new orders.

Edwin Richard's father died in 1911 and he took over the reins of the firm. He was the first to use pneumatic tyres on a steam wagon and developed a number of very advanced designs but the authorities were anti-steam and he began to investigate diesel power at the end of the 1920s. His colleagues on the board were not interested and so, for both business and health reasons, he retired to Blackpool in 1930. He was not inactive, however, and pondered deeply on the possibilities of diesel. Then, in 1932, he began to construct his own prototype diesel lorry in a rented shed back at Sandbach with the assistance of

former Foden colleagues and son Dennis. Carrying the legend 'E R Foden & Son Diesel', the first ERF, as it was soon known, was well ahead of its time and a new factory was set up almost immediately with E R Foden as Managing Director.

Business built up rapidly and E R Foden remained an active participant until his death in 1950.

FORD, Henry *(1863-1947)*
Born the son of Irish immigrants in Wayne County, Michigan, on 30 July 1863, Henry Ford started his working life as a machinist's apprentice in Detroit at the age of 15. He soon moved back to the family farm and set up a small machine shop and sawmill, determined to make farm work a lot easier.

His persistence won him the post of Chief Engineer to the Edison Co, Detroit, which he held until 1899 when he set up the Detroit Automobile Co with some colleagues but left soon after to construct racing cars. This led to the formation of the Ford Motor Co in 1903 and the introduction of the immortal Model 'T' five years later. Ford soon earned himself a reputation for revolutionizing production techniques, his philosophy being to produce as many vehicles as possible and by so doing cut the price to the customer. By 1913 the Model 'T' was selling at just $500 and when discontinued in 1927 was replaced by the Model 'A'. A V8 petrol engine was developed in 1932 and gradually the company opened plants throughout the world, all employing mass-production techniques.

LEVASSOR, Emile *(1844-1897)*
Emile Levassor was a French inventor who, with René Panhard, took over a manufacturer of woodworking machinery in 1886 and began building his own version of the Daimler petrol engine for the French market on behalf

Gottlieb W. Daimler

of a Belgian entrepreneur. Unfortunately, this gentleman died suddenly so Levassor married his widow to whom the French Daimler rights had passed. He developed a revolutionary new car layout with horizontal engine ahead of the driver to provide good front wheel adhesion and a pinion-and-gearwheel transmission providing several alternative speeds. Such a layout was to become the norm for both cars and commercials of the immediate future.

Edwin R. Foden

MORRIS, William R *(1877-1963)*
Born in Worcestershire in October 1877, William Richard Morris was forced to give up his hopes of a medical career through his father's ill-health, beginning work at 15 by setting up a cycle repair shop behind his home. He also built cycles to order and raced them, later moving on to motorcycles and finally to cars. In 1903 he took a partner into the business but was soon bankrupt.

With a set of tools and a £50 debt, he established a small workshop at Cowley, Oxford, where he constructed the first Morris 'Oxford' 2-seater in 1913. Prosperity followed and he soon introduced the Morris 'Cowley', assembling this along Ford's mass-production lines. Morris Motors Ltd was founded in 1919 and in order to survive during 1920/1 all prices were slashed drastically. In 1923 his Morris Garages operation constructed the first MG and in the same year he formed Morris Commercial Cars Ltd to introduce mass-production techniques into the British truck industry.

In 1952 his vehicle-building activities were merged with those of the Austin Motor Co Ltd to form the British Motor Corp, which at the time was the third largest vehicle manufacturer in the world.

OLDS, Ransom E *(1864-1950)*
Claimed to be the first successful American vehicle manufacturer,

Ransom Eli Olds was born at Geneva, Ohio, in 1864 and as a young man quickly established a reputation as a first-rate inventor. His first 3hp curved-dash Olds appeared in the 1890s and in 1899 he established the Olds Motor Works, backed financially by Samuel L Smith, in Lansing, Michigan, to construct Oldsmobile cars on one of the world's first automotive assembly lines.

Unfortunately, a disagreement with Smith led to Old's resignation in 1904 after which he found the Reo Motor Car Co, the descendant of which was to become world-famous as a heavy truck producer.

SELDEN, George B *(1846-1922)*
Fully qualified as a lawyer, George Baldwin Selden, born 1846, was granted a patent for a revolutionary road engine in 1895 and sold the rights to this only on a royalty basis. For a while he had the entire American motor industry eating out of his hand but his monopoly was brought to an end by Henry Ford who stubbornly refused to pay. Selden took him to court and in a 1911 decision it was decreed that the Ford design was fundamentally different and royalties did not have to be paid.

SIMMS, Frederick R *(1863-1935)*
Frederick Richard Simms, born in 1863, was one of the great pioneers of the British motor industry, founding Simms & Co, consulting engineers, in 1890, which pioneered the use of low-tension

Frederick R. Simms

ignitions and the manufacture of motorboat engines and aerial cableways.

In 1901 Simms founded the Society of Motor Manufacturers & Traders, and was elected its first President. As well as building both cars and commercials in the early days, Simms's company concentrated on the manufacture of vehicle ignition systems and fuel-injection equipment during the 1930s but he resigned his position of Managing Director in 1935 and died nine years later.

A powerful GMC Astro hauls a
heavy load on one of the many
super-highways of the USA.

MOTORCYCLES

ERWIN TRAGATSCH

Triumphant moment . . . the author worked for the British firm in the 1950s

The word *motorcycle* was first used to describe a bicycle with an internal combustion engine in 1893; although the first bicycle with an engine had appeared some 20 years earlier, it was powered by steam, and it was not until the advent of the petrol engine that a successful motorcycle was made. The idea spread rapidly, motorcycles soon became widely available in Europe and America, and a new and popular means of transport had arrived.

Motorcycles, An Illustrated History describes the wordwide development of the motorcycle from those pioneering days to the advanced technology of the 1970s. The opening chapter deals with the development of the industry from the early machines produced by Hildebrand and Wolfmüller to the post-Second World War success story of Japanese technology. The history of the motorcycle is then traced from the pioneer years of the 1890s, through the machines developed during the First World War and the post-war boom during the 1920s to the designs which appeared during the Second World War. There is a chapter on the great designers, and the book concludes with details of the classics superbly illustrated in full colour: here are the Henderson and the Harley-Davidson, the Scott and the Brough Superior, the Ducati Desmo and the Yamaha twins – the all-time classic machines through the decades.

THE STORY OF AN INDUSTRY

THE HISTORY of the motorcycle also offers a short course in design philosophy and industrial economics, with some politics thrown in.

Great pioneers like Hildebrand and Wolfmüller were clever inventors, but their design went into production without any development work. The result was that the factory went broke in a very few years. The same fate befell Colonel H. C. L. Holden's 'moto-bicycle', which had four horizontal watercooled cylinders directly driving the rear wheel. This, too, was an ingenious design, but was already obsolete before it would have gone into quantity production in 1900. In France, the Russian-born Werner brothers, Michael and Eugene, built a motorcycle to a design using De Dion proprietary engines from 52 to 70mm bore and always a 70mm stroke. The 70/70 model built in 1899 had 2·25 hp (269cc). These were smaller and lighter engines than had been used before. After 1902, they used strengthened bicycle frames, mounting the engine above the pedalling gear, and this machine became the ancestor of motorcycles as we know them today.

A practical basic design had been established, but the story of the motorcycle continued to be a story of designers and technicians who sometimes had no commercial sense. There were also designs which worked briefly but which look strange to modern eyes: the German Megola, designed by Fritz Cockerell, was clutchless and gearless, and had to be started by being pushed. It would be hopelessly impractical, and even dangerous, in modern traffic, but more than 2000 of them were sold in the 1920s.

The founders of the great motorcycle factories had to be visionary men of great technical ability and with no small amount of idealism. The profit margin in this developing competitive business was usually lower than that in other industries. It often happened that when the founder died or retired, the factory went into decline, being managed by industrialists rather than motorcycle men: a good example of this was the Indian factory at Springfield, Massachusetts. In 1912, Indian was one of the largest motorcycle factories in the world, employing about 3,000 people on three shifts. When founder George M. Hendee retired in the mid-1920s, the factory began a long, slow decline. When it was finally bought in 1959 by Associated Motor Cycles Ltd., of London, the only thing left was the Indian name on motorcycles produced for the American market.

Designers were often people who wanted to sell their designs to others, and get on with something new. They were often less interested in the continuous development of a machine once it was in production. So it was that William Henderson created his big four-cylinder aircooled Henderson, sold it and went on to design the not dissimilar Ace. After Henderson's death in an accident in 1922, it was Arthur Lemon who continued development work on the Henderson for Ignaz Schwinn's Chicago-based bicycle company. On the other hand, sometimes a good design has been developed but basically unchanged for many years because of its intrinsic excellence: the best example of this is the famous BMW twin. Since the machine was first shown in Paris in 1923, BMW has never built a twin which was not horizontally opposed, mounted transversely in the frame and which did not drive a shaft rather than a chain. The original designer was Max Friz.

The motorcycle industry, like any other, is also subject to factors outside its control. A great many factories went under during the Great Depression of the 1930s, to say nothing of the German hyper-inflation of 1923. After each of the two world wars, motorcycles were in such short supply that small companies sprang up in every country, doing well for a short time with designs which in many cases were essentially undistinguished. When Hitler gobbled up Central Europe in the late 1930s, some small producers of motorcycles disappeared because they could not be fitted into the Nazis' industrial plans.

By contrast, the Italian motorcycle industry has broken nearly every rule in the book: before the Second World War, the Italians built good machines, but did not try very hard to export them; since the war, while the Italian economy may have experienced its vicissitudes, a surprising number of relatively small producers, as well as a few big ones, have managed to stay in business. They have also continued to uphold the traditional Italian reputation for good design. There has been no lack of great designers in the Italian industry: Carlo Guzzi's designs in developed form

The 1920s was the boom period for the small manufacturer, though producers like BMW (left, top) had already adopted a methodical approach. Half a century later, the masters of the production line are the Japanese, with Kawasaki (bottom picture) among the leaders.

became the famous Albatross racers. Angelo Parodi, Giulo Carcano and Lino Tonti also helped to design the Moto Guzzi machines; in the mid-1950s, Carcano was designing four-cylinder and V-8 double-ohc racing machines. In the late 1950s, very fine Bianchi double-ohc vertical twins were designed by Tonti, who then went on to create transverse-mounted V-twins with shaft drive for Moto Guzzi. The six Benelli brothers and many others have contributed to the excellence of Italian machines; yet today, even the Italian industry is falling victim to the post-war trend towards industrial conglomeration.

The saddest story of all is the decline of the British motorcycle industry, for decades the world's leader. The incompetence of management, and of various governments, has seen the British motorcycle industry lose its leadership by default. For one thing, it is not possible to stay in the motorcycle business on any sizable scale unless a wide range of models is offered. In the face of Japanese competition, British factories gave up the mass-production of small machines; for some years thereafter, British superbikes were still very popular, but it was no longer economically feasible to build them.

The Japanese deserve their success, there can be no doubt about that. The Honda factory has stayed on top because it has been ready to re-invest its profits in up-to-date plant and equipment, and because Soichiro Honda does not need weeks or months of consultation with banks, Boards of Directors and numerous unions before making a decision. The character of designing has also changed: if Mike Mizumachi is responsible for the

brilliant success of the Kawasaki factory, it is also true that he has not done it single-handedly, but is the head of a brilliant team of younger men who will no doubt become famous in their own right. Times have changed. The motorcycle business is no different from any other; only people who can change with the times can stay on top.

The motorcycle factories which survived the Great Depression were those which were large and strong, and which already had networks of dealers and customers dependent on a good name for service, spare parts and so forth. The day of the committed idealist who could start his own factory on a shoe-string was past. Designers became less freelance geniuses and more valued employees of established manufacturers. Even before the Second World War, the process of combination began in which, for example, Matchless swallowed AJS to become Associated Motor Cycles which in turn took over Francis Barnett, James, Norton – and even the American Indian factory after WWII.

In the post-war years this process accelerated, until it actually became uneconomic to build motorcycles in countries with high per-capita incomes. In the 1920s, there were perhaps fifteen different companies building very good machines in the USA; eventually only Harley-Davidson was left. Even Harley had to buy the Italian Aermacchi works in order to produce comparatively small machines at competitive prices. Small countries such as The Netherlands, Belgium, Denmark and Switzerland once had notable indigenous producers; today motorcycle production in these countries is virtually nil. Nations such as Italy and Spain, which have the

design and engineering skill but which are relatively undeveloped, have thriving motorcycle industries because they are economically competitive.

The special cases are Socialist countries, such as Czechoslovakia and East Germany. Whatever else one might say about nationalized industry, these countries produce their own two-wheeled transport and they have no unemployment to speak of. Another special case is Britain, the world's leader for decades; during the 1950s, British imports spelled the end of much American competition in the industry. Yet today Britain's industry is almost finished. It is perhaps not too much to say that part of Britain's problem is that it can't decide what kind of economics it wants; certainly the measures it has taken in the motorcycle industry are half-measures. Britain has the skills, and with the fall of the Pound it should be economically competitive; one can only hope that it will have a Renaissance of spirit.

The overwhelming factor in the post-war motorcycle industry has been Japan. In 1970, Britain built about 64,500 machines; Germany built about 70,000, and Japan built nearly three million. The fact that Japan has beaten the Western countries at their own game, and in a very short time, is a tribute to her industry and her single-mindedness. Once we regarded factories with a yearly production of 20,000 machines as 'bigger'. But in 1981 the four Japanese motorcycle producers—Honda, Yamaha, Suzuki and Kawasaki—built 7,412,582 machines between them and up to the end of April 1982 they had built 2,633,307 motorcycles overall. A few years ago such figures were thought impossible.

MOTORCYCLE PRODUCTION IN MAIN MANUFACTURING NATIONS

Country	1969	1970	1971	1972	1973	1974	1975	1976	1977	1978	1979	1980	1981
Austria	4,278	7,044	7,643	11,768	12,253	14,244	10,746	11,119	9,006	7,629	8,613	10,539	9,482
England	71,010	64,521	86,650	48,832	48,439	40,000		18,900	14,400	23,900	16,600	11,600	3,100
Czechoslovakia				270,000			118,566	110,557	108,954			136,000	
France	3,375	4,292	6,508	6,627	8,686	9,038	8,513	5,510	7,463	3,680	4,310	1,505	5,097
Germany	52,568	70,123	66,462	69,099	84,357	66,901	74,660	73,356	79,032	59,637	58,521	49,494	88,315
Italy	580,000	560,000	617,000	682,500	694,500	795,500	833,000	246,500	280,500	332,500	310,600	402,750	484,550
Japan	2,576,873	2,947,672	3,400,502	3,565,246	3,767,327	4,509,420	3,802,547	4,235,112	5,577,359	5,999,929	4,475,956	6,434,524	7,412,582
Spain	32,514	30,437	36,661	49,465	54,176	59,747	58,351	52,122	63,379	59,284	52,371	39,394	35,732

THE PIONEER YEARS

IT IS IMPOSSIBLE to bestow on any individual the credit for having 'invented' the motorcycle. There was much preliminary development to be accomplished before any kind of motor vehicle could be practical.

In 1876, Nikolaus August Otto built a four-stroke internal combustion engine. Dugald Clerk, in 1877-78, developed a two-stroke compression machine with a charging pump. In 1883, Gottlieb Daimler and Wilhelm Maybach invented surface ignition, which made possible a fast-running lightweight engine. Otto invented a low-tension make-and-break (coil) ignition in 1884, and the next year Daimler and Maybach built a two-wheeled vehicle with a wooden frame and belt drive. Finally, in 1894 Heinrich Hildebrand and Alois Wolfmüller designed the first commercially-built two-wheeler to be called a motorcycle.

In 1895 there were French three-wheelers using the De Dion engines, such as the Gladiator, and in England the Beeston. The year 1896 saw the quantity manufacture of these engines, and in 1897 the Werner machine appeared in Paris with the engine above the front wheel. Soon, the Werners also had a factory in London. The Coventry Motor Company was building machines in the city of the same name, in the industrial Midlands of England. In the same city, Humber and Beeston were in production. In the same year, Italy's Edoardo Bianchi commenced production. In 1898, the factory of Georges Bouton and Count De Dion began production of a three-wheeler, using their own 239cc engine.

De Dion engines were extremely successful. By 1899, they had overtaken the Hildebrand and Wolfmüller design; in that year, Laurin and Klement began motorcycle production in what was then the Austro-Hungarian Empire, using the 239cc De Dion engine until they developed their own. Engines were also being made by Sarolea in Belgium, and a clever Frenchman called André Boudeville began manufacture of high-tension magnetos in Paris. 1899 also saw the first 211cc Minerva engine, the first engine-assisted Raleigh bicycles, the first Matchless motorcycles

Early days in France and Germany . . . Above: the first Daimler and Maybach two-wheeler (left) and the 1894 Hildebrand & Wolfmüller. Bottom: the Parisian Werner Motorcyclette, and the De Dion-Bouton three-wheeler. T. Tessier broke a speed record on an English BAT (right) in 1903.

THOSE MAGNIFICENT MEN ON THEIR CYCLING MACHINES

A steam engine, fired by petrol, powered this von Sauerbronn-Davis velocipede, 1883

The 1887 Millet prototype had a radial engine similar to those later used in aircraft

Propellor power . . . a chitty, chitty, bang bike by Anzani had its test flight in 1906

Look, no pedals! An ordinary bicycle gets a shove from an auxiliary engine . . . Italy, 1893

'Luxurious, high-powered, all-weather car-ette'
. . . twin engined Quadrant, made in Britain, 1905

Where to put the engine? Above the front wheel, perhaps? That (1) was Werner's solution, in 1899. Enfield placed the engine in the same place, but to drive the rear wheel

Strange layouts abounded at the turn of the century . . . Singer positioned the engine in the hub of the front wheel (2). Further variations came from British Excelsior (3), Phelon and Moore (4), Hildebrand and Wolfmüller (5), Beeston (6), Ormonde (7), Singer again (8) and Humber (9).

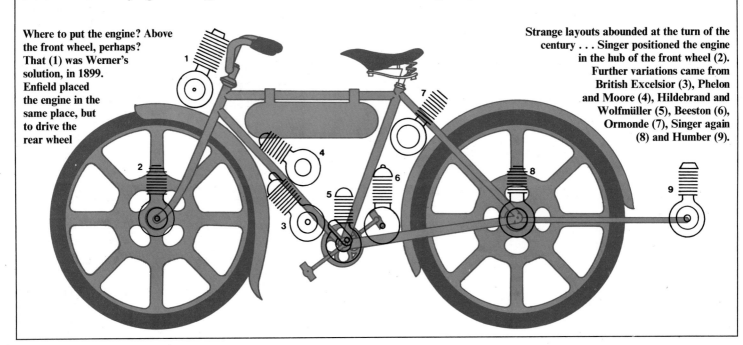

and the first motorcycle races: at the Friedenauer Cycle Track in Germany and the Exelberg in Austria.

The first year of the new century brought the introduction of the Perks & Birch (later Singer) motor wheel, Joah Phelon's first P&M motorcycle, the first Excelsiors built by Bayliss-Thomas, and in America, the Orient motorcycle designed by Charles H. Metz. In 1901, Swedish-American Oscar Hedström built the first Indian motorcycle, and the Werners experimented with vertical engines mounted in the centre of the frame. Puch and NSU built their first motorcycles, the latter using the Swiss Zedel engine. In England, Yorkshire's Alfred Angas Scott began the development of his unorthodox two-stroke engines, which are still famous today. Also in 1901, Orient became the first American company to export a machine to Europe. Emil Hafelfinger, also an American, created the first two-speed gear, and Condor, a Swiss factory, began producing motorized bicycles.

Also in Switzerland, the Dufaux brothers began producing bicycle attachment engines, calling their product Motosacoche (engine in the pocket). The same factory later produced the MAG engine, playing the same part on the Continent as JAP (J. A. Prestwich & Co. Ltd.) in England, who began producing proprietary engines in 1902. (The Swiss factory always made complete machines as well, but the London factory after 1908 made engines only.) The year also saw the manufacture of ohv engines by the French Clément works, Strickland's design of vertical twins, and Ariel's first motorcycles, built in Birmingham with Belgian Kerry engines. Wicker sidecars were being made by Mills & Fulford in Coventry.

The aircooled four-cylinder FN, with shaft drive, came into quantity production in 1903. Another four was built by Charles Binks, and Buchet in France was supplying a vertical twin with no less than 4245cc capacity. Shaft-driven singles were built by FN and by William Starley. White & Poppe began building 3 hp single-cylinder proprietary engines. America saw the first Harley-Davidson motorcycle, made in Milwaukee, Wisconsin. Triumph, in Britain, began making their own engines; with the help of Bettmann and Schulte, the two Germans who had come to Coventry to found Triumph, the German

In Czechoslovakia, Laurin & Klement produced the elegant single-cylinder B–D in 1903 (top), and more sporting versions such as the V-twin CCR (below). Bottom: Ludwig Opel with a 2¾ hp Opel motorcycle on army manoeuvres in 1905.

company of the same name began to build motorcycles in Nuremberg. The British BAT machine had a spring frame; the factory at Penge was owned by the Tessier family. It was widely thought that BAT stood for 'best after test', but the designer's name was Batson.

In France the Bichrone two-stroke was installed in Griffon frames. In 1904 the International Coupé Race in France became the first international motorcycle event. Demester of France won it riding a Griffon; number two was Toman riding a Laurin & Klement. Automatic inlet valves became common on engines and Peugeot of France now used Truffault's swinging arm forks. Dürkopp and Laurin & Klement built four-in-line engines. While England had 21,521 machines registered, only 776 were exported. Hercules and Victoria of Germany entered the market, and a Peugeot rider reached 76·5 mph on a machine weighing 110 pounds.

The following year, 1905, saw the introduction in England of quantity production of Scott's, not yet at the famous works in Shipley, Yorkshire, but at the Jowett works in nearby Bradford. Another new make was the Fairy, with a horizontally opposed twin designed by J. Barter. This was the forerunner of the Douglas. There were more vertical twins, too; the Belgian Bercley designed by Gustave Kindermann and Eugene Werner's own Werner, built in Paris. Both the Werner brothers, great pioneers of motorcycling, died the same year.

There was a switch to magneto ignition by most factories in 1906. In that year the

The start of the first T.T. race in 1908 (inset, far left), and the 1908 twin-cylinder class winner Harry Reed astride his D.O.T. Big picture: the circuit's notorious Devil's Elbow. Bottom: winner of the 1905 International Coupe, Václav Vondřich on a Laurin & Klement Type CCR.

British firm of JAP built the first ohv V-twin engines. A JAP engine powered the first three-cylinder Dennell, from Yorkshire. The same county produced the P&M, which had a two-speed gear, with clutch. The year 1906 also saw the first Druid spring forks. The year before, Václav Vondřich, riding a Laurin & Klement V-twin, had won the Coupé International, but in 1906 it was the Austrian Edward Nikodem, on a Puch.

After this race, British riders complained about the bad organisation, and mainly about the interpretation of the rules by certain Continental teams. After their return they decided to start their own event, and the result was the first Tourist Trophy race in the Isle of Man. This was in 1907, the same year that a trade slump caused the disappearance of some motorcycle producers. Glenn Curtis, an American manufacturer of aircraft engines, allegedly reached an unofficial 130 mph using a modified transverse-mounted V-8. Douglas had started quantity production of their machines with the Barter-designed flat-twin engine, and Eysink in Holland introduced their own vertical twins. 1908 saw the opening of Brooklands, the famous racetrack at Weybridge, south of London. It also saw the first Italian entrant in the TT race, riding an English Rex. A new design by the Dufaux brothers had a seven-cylinder rotary engine built into the rear wheel. This was the first and last seven ever built.

Triumphs in England got hub clutches in their rear wheels in 1909, a very good design by Maurice Schulte. That year also saw the P. G. Tacchi-designed Wilkinson TAC (Touring Auto Cycle, with a steering wheel) which soon became the TMC (Touring Motor Cycle, with handlebars). Both had aircooled (or optionally watercooled) four-in-line engines, and both were built by the Wilkinson Sword Company, later famous for razor blades. The Stevens brothers began manufacture of complete motorcycles called AJS. Renouf's James design was interesting, with its chassis-type frame and a spring seat pillar. Giuseppe Gilera's was a new make. At Brooklands, an NLG (North London Garages) reached 90 mph with an ohv V-twin of 2713cc built by JAP. The rider was W. E. Cook. F. A. McNab broke the one-hour record riding a Trump, which also had a JAP engine. McNab was one of the owners of the Trump factory.

A motorcycle boom started in 1910, but didn't help the new Renouf-designed James, a horizontally-opposed two-stroke twin with overheating problems. Britain had exported £24,202 worth of motorcycles in 1909, and more than doubled it in 1910 to £53,661. The boom in the USA resulted in 86,414 registrations. In Britain, Zenith's Fred Barnes designed the famous Gradua gear and a spring frame.

In 1911 the American Indian machines scored a 1-2-3 victory in the Senior TT, the biggest shock for the British industry

The T.T. attracted competitors from many countries. Here the Bianchi team of 1926 pose with their fast 348cc dohc singles including the manufacturer Edoardo Bianchi (with cap), and on his right Miro Maffeis, Mario Ghersi and—sitting on the machine—Luigi Arcangeli. The Indian 'Hendee Special' of 1914 (bottom) was the first motorcycle with an electric self-starter.

until the Japanese invasion of the 1960s. The Indians were ridden by O. C. Godfrey, C. B. Franklin and A. J. Moorhouse. Rudge (Rudge Whitworth) came onto the scene that year with a 499cc single which had overhead-inlet and side-exhaust valves and which afterwards got the well-known Multi gear. Britain's motorcycle exports rose to the value of £120,289 and Charlie Collier—one of the three brothers of Matchless fame—broke the official world record with 91·37 mph. In France, Meuriot rode a Rene-Gillet at the Gomez-le-Chatel hill climb. The machine had a cross-shaped four-cylinder 20 hp engine which was really a radial. John Wooler built his first machine: a 346cc two-stroke with a horizontal cylinder and an additional pumping piston in the crankcase. (The same John Wooler was designing four-cylinder machines 40 years later, after the Second World War.) 1911 was also a busy year in America, with Bill Henderson creating his aircooled four-in-line, Pope building 498cc singles and 996cc ohv V-twins, and Jack Prince building a famous racetrack at Los Angeles.

Sunbeam machines entered the market in 1912. Designed by J. E. Greenwood and built at Wolverhampton in the West Midlands of England, they were of outstanding design and quality, among the finest machines ever built. Also from Wolverhampton came the Villiers proprietary engines, which in those far-off days were four-strokes, not the two-strokes we knew so well later. During this period, the Indian factory was a busy, thriving place, and the Italian Bianchi factory was the same. In 1912, founder Edoardo Bianchi

at the age of 45 was made a *Cavaliere del Lavoro*. Alas, Sunbeam, Indian and Bianchi are all gone today.

C. B. Redrup designed his first three-cylinder radial engine in 1912; Rex in Coventry and others built two-speed countershafts in front of the engines; ASL, a spring factory, built motorcycles with spring frames. In races, Charlie and Harry Collier of Matchless fame used new six-speed gearboxes. At Brooklands, they got more American competition in the form of H. A. Shaw on a 7 hp Thor and J. E. Hogge on a 4 hp Indian. A boost for two-strokes came in the Isle of Man, when Frank Applebee won the Senior TT on a 3·5 hp Scott with an average speed of 48·70 mph, and the fastest lap with 49·44 mph. G. E.

Stanley's hour record at Brooklands stood until 1920.

The Americans went on and on. Harley-Davidsons got chain drive to replace the belt drive; Indian supplied some models with full electrical equipment, a rarity in those days. In 1913 Andrew Strand designed with John McNeill the first commercially-built 996cc ohc V-twin, the Cyclone, and many were sold to private sportsmen in the USA.

Technically, the most outstanding motorcycle of 1913 was the 494cc vertical twin Peugeot racing machine, designed by Antoinescu, but based on the Peugeot racing car engine design of 1912. This double-ohc engine was re-designed many times and was still winning races in 1927; it was never sold to private entrants. Triumph in England experimented with a vertical twin, and Humber with a three-cylinder model, but they never went into quantity production. A new English sporting event, the International Sixdays Trial, was introduced and is still with us. Russia was in the news when a rider from that country participated in the Senior TT; his name was Kremleff. He rode a Rudge and retired after a crash.

Britain had by this time 179,926 registered motorcycles, the Americans produced 70,000 machines in 1913 and Carl Goudy, riding an American Schwinn-built Excelsior, won the 100 mile race at Columbus. A new Indian was the 2·25 hp two-stroke 211cc machine.

THE FIRST WORLD WAR

As THE 1914 WAR BROKE OUT in Europe, the Chicago-based Schwinn-owned Excelsior Company moved to new works at 3700 Cortland Street. Glen Boyd won on an Indian the first race at Dodge City. In Britain. Cyril Pullin on a Rudge and Eric Williams on an sv AJS won the last pre-first-war Senior and Junior TT races. Jack Emerson took an ABC with a Bradshaw-designed 496cc flat-twin engine to Brooklands and got a speed of 80·47 mph. Despite the world political situation, the British motorcycle industry exported 20,877 motorcycles. Puch, the Austrian factory, built machines with horizontally opposed cylinders. Burman in England, famous for gears and gearboxes, entered the manufacture of proprietary engines, but the war prevented their mass production.

Motorcycles played an important part in the war. The British used mainly Triumph, Douglas, P&M, Clyno and Sunbeams: the Germans NSU and Wanderer machines; the French René Gillets, the Austrians Puchs and the Italians Bianchis and a variety of other makes. Britain supplied machines to the Czar of Russia, including Rovers and Premiers. A cargo of 250 Premier machines was sunk in the North Sea on its way to Russia.

Premier built in 1915 the prototype of a new 322cc two-stroke vertical twin. For two years they developed it, but never began quantity production. It was in fact the last Premier ever made in Coventry; soon after the war, the factory was bought by Singer. Also new was a 90-degree V-twin, made by Phelon & Moore at Cleckheaton, in Yorkshire, the works which supplied many singles to the British Air Force during the war. Like the Premier, it

During the First World War, the American Forces ordered 70,000 Harleys, some rigged as armed outfits (above). Britain had a Clyno-Vickers machine-gun outfit (below).

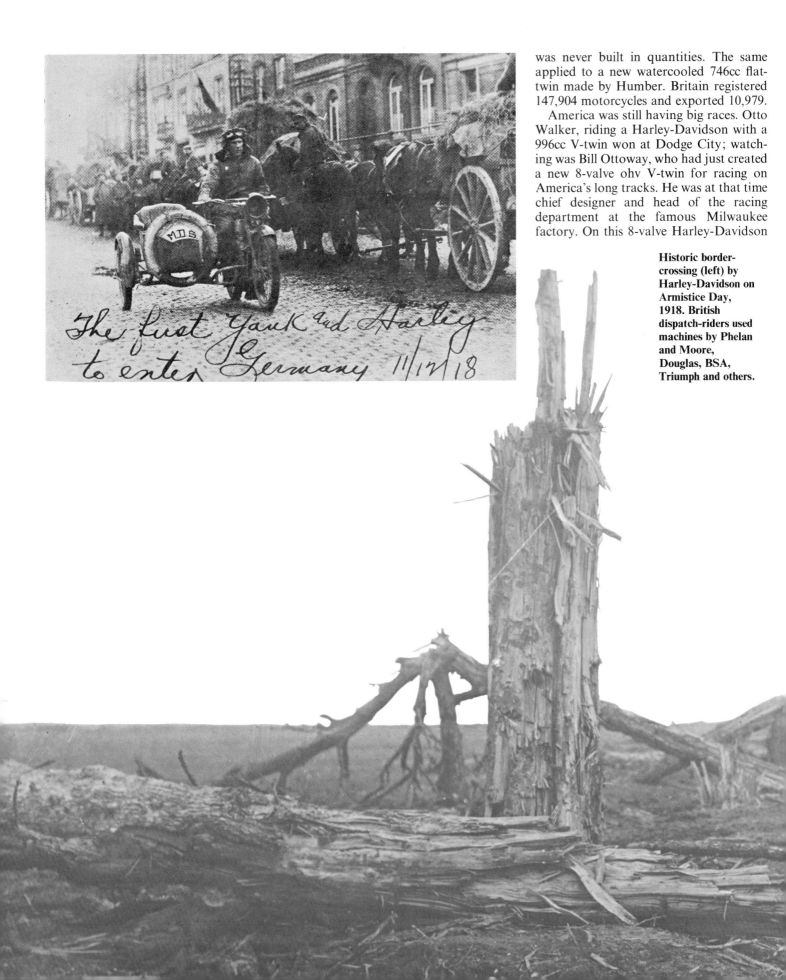

The first Yank and Harley to enter Germany 11/12/18

was never built in quantities. The same applied to a new watercooled 746cc flat-twin made by Humber. Britain registered 147,904 motorcycles and exported 10,979.

America was still having big races. Otto Walker, riding a Harley-Davidson with a 996cc V-twin won at Dodge City; watching was Bill Ottoway, who had just created a new 8-valve ohv V-twin for racing on America's long tracks. He was at that time chief designer and head of the racing department at the famous Milwaukee factory. On this 8-valve Harley-Davidson

Historic border-crossing (left) by Harley-Davidson on Armistice Day, 1918. British dispatch-riders used machines by Phelan and Moore, Douglas, BSA, Triumph and others.

German dispatch-rider (below, left), in W.W.I. His machine was a 604cc Wanderer V-twin. Below right: British rider on a 547cc BSA photographed in 1917 during the German East Africa campaign.

Jack Janke was the winner at Dodge City in 1916. In the same year, William Hendee —the founder of Indian at Springfield— sold most of his shares in the factory; Roy Artley, riding a four-cylinder Henderson, broke the Los Angeles to San Francisco record with 10 hours and 4 minutes and Britain's number of motorcycles stood, despite the war, at 153,000.

Motorcycle prices increased during the war; even in the USA one had to pay the equivalent of £170 for a 269cc two-stroke Cleveland. That was in 1917, when Indian built the first 996cc Powerplus V-twins, the 15 hp Thor V-twin got a reverse gear, Excelsior in Chicago bought the Henderson design and Harley-Davidson got a big Army order for their machines. In 1918, nearly all factories in the world worked for the war. Some prepared for peace; others were anxious because when the war was over they would lose valuable government contracts.

THE 1920s...THE GOLDEN AGE

THE FIRST YEAR OF PEACE saw much activity in the motorcycle industry. There was such a demand for machines that many factories switched over to the assembly or manufacture of motorcycles, without having the necessary experience or suitable equipment. Second-class machines, and even really bad ones, found customers, until the market was quite satisfied and buyers of motorcycles could tell good designs from bad ones. It was a technically interesting, but commercially unstable period. There were many producers which arrived from nowhere and soon disappeared, leaving behind unhappy customers and problems.

The year 1919 saw the introduction of a good two-stroke single, the 497cc Dunelt with the double-diameter piston, which created a certain amount of forced induction. In the USA appeared the first Bill Henderson-designed four-in-line ACE, which eventually became in 1927 the first Indian four. In Germany a new make, DKW, became famous for good two-strokes. The first one was designed by the very experienced Hugo Ruppe, who was also the creator of Bekamo two-strokes, which had wooden frames and a pumping piston in the crankcase for forced induction. Bekamos were to win many races in the early 1920s. Another new creation was the Bradshaw-designed 398cc ABC with the transverse-mounted flat-twin ohv engine, produced by the Sopwith Engineering Co. It was a modern conception, but was not fully developed when it was put on the market. Sunbeam became part of the Nobel (ICI) group.

In Italy, the 346cc Garelli with the double-piston two-stroke single-cylinder engine was another make which soon after the war gained popularity and successes in sporting events. Adalberto Garelli created this unorthodox design. A short-lived scooter boom swamped England. Alfred Angus Scott had sold his interests in the now Shipley-based Scott Motorcycle Company. The new make Francis Barnett bought the Bayliss-Thomas works at Coventry, after Bayliss-Thomas — manufacturers of English Excelsior motorcycles — had moved to Birmingham. The other Excelsior factory — owned by Ignaz Schwinn at Chicago — built new John McNeill-designed motorcycles with ohc racing engines (498cc and 996cc) for the works team, while Charles Franklin crea-

ted the famous 596cc sv V-twin Scout for Indian, one of the finest machines ever made in the USA. Franklin, an Irishman, had been one of the winners in the 1911 Senior TT.

A very interesting machine, the German Mars, was designed in 1920 by Franzenberg. It had a frame made from pressed steel plates which were welded and rivetted together.

The Mars' power unit was the only motorcycle engine ever built by the famous Maybach car and aero-engine works at Friedrichshafen. It had two horizontally-opposed cylinders, a capacity of 956cc and side valves. Starting was by a crank. This design was produced for nearly ten years in slightly developed form. And there was a motorcycle boom in nearly all countries; Britain had 280,000 registered machines, produced by nearly 200 different assemblers and manufacturers. A new design was a 248cc V-twin made by Diamond, but it never went into quantity production. The first official world speed record for motorcycles was established on April 14, 1920 by Ernie Walker at Daytona on a 994cc V-twin Indian with more than 101 mph. Racing in America was again in full swing and the leading factories such as

Indian, Harley-Davidson, Excelsior (including Henderson) and Reading-Standard competed in most events. Dodge City was won by Jim Davis on a Harley-Davidson, where there was a new flat-twin of 584cc with side-valves designed by Bill Ottoway.

Many new makes and models appeared in 1921. It was the year of the first Carlo Guzzi-designed 497cc Moto-Guzzi, with a horizontal single-cylinder ioe engine, and the first George Brough-designed 974cc Brough-Superior V-twin with a JAP engine. At Munich, the first Megola — the Fritz Cockerell-designed machine with a 5-cylinder radial engine of 640cc built directly into the front wheel — appeared on the scene. It had neither clutch nor gearbox. Around 2000 were built when after four years the factory closed down. It was also 1921 when Hugo Ruppe, who had created the first DKW, began manufacture of his own 129cc Bekamos. The same year, Sun in England used 269cc and afterwards 247cc Vitesse engines, two-strokes with a rotary valve on the induction side. Harry Ricardo, later Sir Harry Ricardo, was busy at Triumph in Coventry, developing his excellent 498cc ohv four-valve single-cylinder 'Riccy' model. Barr & Stroud of Glasgow began manufacture of 347cc sleeve-valve proprietary engines. Scotts got saddle-tanks. Scooters began to disappear, but motorcycles sold like hot cakes, despite the very high prices. Some examples: 247cc Levis two-stroke, £65; 799cc V-twin AJS with sidecar, £210; 748cc four-cylinder FN with shaft drive, £160; 490cc Norton with sv engine, £132.

Belgium had its first Grand Prix motorcycle race in 1921 and Ernst Neumann-Neander, the well-known German designer, created a prototype with an Adler-built 123cc engine. Italy had a TT race in 1921 at the Circuito del Lario and Amedeo Ruggeri — in the 1930s a Maserati racing-car driver — won it on a 998cc Harley-Davidson. The year's registration figure in the UK: 373,200; in the USA: 154,000. New in 1921 also was a 596cc V-twin Bianchi from Italy and a similar 494cc version made by Galloni; Benelli entered the market with a 98cc two-stroke. The V-twin 477cc Borgo racing machine had 8 valves and ohc, as well as a partly oil-cooled unit-design engine.

The many flat-twins built in 1921 mainly in Britain and Italy included the Fongri,

The post-war years saw a short-lived craze for the scooter (left). The unorthodox 5-cylinder Megola was raced by Toni Bauhofer and reached speeds up to 140 km/h.

Maxima, SAR, Raleigh, Humber, Wooler, Zenith, Dalton, Slaney, Brough, Douglas, Williamson, ABC and also the American Harley-Davidson and Czechoslovakian Itar, as well as the German Victoria, Aristos, SBD, Mars, Astra and more.

The year 1922 saw the last Tourist Trophy success by a British two-stroke, when Geoff Davison on a Levis won the Lightweight race. It saw also the first double-piston 122cc single-cylinder Puch two-stroke, designed by Giovanni Marcel-lino. Blackburne motorcycle production was taken over by Osborne Engineering Company (OEC), but manufacture of proprietary motorcycle engines continued at Burney & Blackburne. The year also saw the introduction of the first Norton with an ohv engine; Rex Judd rode it at Brooklands. New were Val Page-designed 248cc and 348cc ohc racing engines made by JAP while Hubert Hagens, the British Anzani designer, created the successful 998cc V-twin ohc racing engine, which — ridden by Claude Temple — broke many records.

DKW in Germany built the scooter-like Lomos machine, Walter Handley in 1922 rode his first race on an OK Supreme, Dolf in Germany built an eight-port two-stroke and FN of Belgium entered the market with a 347cc ohv single-cylinder machine. Sheffield-Henderson and Coventry-Victors got saddle-tanks and there was for the first time not only a separate Lightweight TT race, but also the first Ulster GP and

'Lawrence of Arabia' (big picture) owned no less than eight Brough-Superior machines. In the bottom picture, from the left, designer and manufacturer George Brough, racer Eddy Meyer and works manager Ike Webb outside the factory in 1927.

at Monza the first Italian Grand Prix. A shaft-driven 498cc Krieger-Gnädig (KG) won the first Avus race at Berlin and a Della Ferrera broke the Italian km record. Interesting, because this works 498cc V-twin had an ohc engine, with chain-driven camshafts; the chains were uncovered and if one takes account of the poor quality of chains in the period, there was a real danger for the rider. This unique design was still seen in 1927 in Italian hill-climbs.

The year 1923 saw the introduction of the first complete 493cc BMW with the transverse-mounted horizontally opposed sv engine, which was already of unit design. This led to the end of proprietary engine production by the Munich factory. Max Friz created the BMW. Less successful than the German factory was Matchless with a new 348cc ohc single, which was never a good racing machine and never really a touring motorcycle either. More interesting was a banking sidecar, used by Freddy Dixon on his Douglas, when winning the 1923 (first ever) sidecar TT race. The same year also saw the first TT race of Amateurs, which eventually became the Manx Grand Prix.

New creations were the A. A. Sidney-designed 348cc ohc Dart and a 398cc BSA prototype, which with its transverse-mounted flat-twin had much in common with the then also new R32 made by BMW. Extremely fast were 144cc and 244cc Hirth two-stroke racers, designed by Helmuth Hirth in Germany. The light-alloy engines were watercooled and of the double-piston variety. Rudge built in 1923 their first ohv models and there was the German Ermag two-stroke, which had a 246cc rotary inlet valve engine, designed by Albert Roder, who created earlier the not unsimilar Ziro. In America, Arthur Lemon took over Henderson design and development from C. Gustafson, while Indian competed for the last time in the Isle of Man TT races. And there was another new TT race; this time in Austria.

The year 1923 was another boom period for motorcycle factories and for manufacturers of proprietary engines as well. The last included the makes JAP, Blackburne, Villiers, Bradshaw, Precision, Coventry-Victor, Broler, Liberty, Dart and on the Continent MAG (Motosacoche), Train, Moser, Zurcher, Chaise, Bekamo, Kühne, Küchen, Baumi, Gruhn, Alba, DKW, Grade etc. A new event in the sporting calendar was the 1000 Mile Stock Trial organised in 1924 by the Auto Cycle Union in England. The year saw also some new designs, including the first ohv BMW model, designed by Rudolf Schleicher, and the new Roconova ohc machines, the first commercially built 248cc and 348cc ohc motorcycles in Germany. Unfortunately Roconova, a design by Johannes Rössig, lasted only three years. In Britain, Connaught bought JES and Brough-Superior introduced Castle forks on the SS100 models, their newest design. Marchant on a Blackburne-engined 348cc Chater-Lea

was the first man officially to break the magic 100 mph limit on a 350cc machine. On April 1, he reached 100·81 mph on a modified 350cc ohc machine. He was a superb designer-tuner as well. Also his friend and opponent Bert le Vack broke records in 1924 and with his 996cc Brough-Superior (ohv JAP) he reached in France over the flying kilometre 119·05 mph, with a one-way run of 122·24 mph. The Americans were fast too and a four-cylinder ACE ridden by Rod Wolverton reached 134 mph. It did not become a world record, as it was not observed officially by the FIM (then still the FICM). The number of registered motorcycles was half a million in England, and British motorcycle exports reached a value of £2,000,000; it was still a period of British supremacy. For Garelli 1924 was a very successful year and the double-piston two-strokes of 348cc won many races against strong opposition. Scott in England was now headed by R. A. Vinter.

Among new machines in 1925 were the 497cc Sunbeam works racers with ohc engines, which never went into quantity production. More successful were the new Italian 348cc Bianchis with double ohc engines, which were nearly unbeatable in Italy until 1931. Velocette in England had a new 348cc ohc single, which was designed by Percy Goodmann and which eventually won races all over the world. New makes were HRD and McEvoy, among others. DKW in Germany produced new water-cooled 173cc racing two-strokes with a charging cylinder at the bottom of the crankcase. The first Dutch TT was run at Assen. A team of very fast 124cc two-stroke singles from Italy won many events. Wal Handley won three 1925 TT races in the Isle of Man in one year. All his machines were made by Rex Acme and had Blackburne ohv engines. In London an unknown young designer named Edward Turner created a 348cc ohc machine; he joined Ariels in 1927 and 10 years later was head of Triumph. George Brough, who built at Nottingham the most expensive machines in England, introduced spring frames. Stefan and Nikolaus v. Horthy, sons of the Hungarian head of state, rode in many races.

Among the most enthusiastic motorcyclists was King Albert of Belgium, who got his fifth machine in 1925, a Belgian built Jeecy-Vea with a British engine.

Old William Brough built his last flat-twins in 1926, but his son continued producing the famous Brough-Superiors, including a new 996cc ohv V-twin with the 45 hp JAP engine, for which he guaranteed a top speed of 100 mph (160 km/h). Therefore the name for this model: SS100. Out went the German 5-cylinder Megola, and Paul Kelecom, the famous Belgian designer, left the FN works. Garelli machines broke not less than 48 world records and Chater-Lea built the first 347cc ohc singles with face cams. In Germany, Adolf Brudes broke the German 1 km record with 104 mph on a supercharged 498cc Victoria, designed by Gustav Steinlein. Sepp Stelzer won the big Avus race on a BMW. A new TT race in Czechoslovakia was won by Rupert Karner of Austria on a 497cc ohv double-port Sunbeam, made in England.

Richard Küchen created new 348cc and 498cc face cam ohc proprietary engines, while DKW—then the biggest motorcycle factory in the world—also supplied 124cc, 127cc, 173cc and 206cc two-stroke deflector-type three-port engines to many motorcycle assemblers. Indian and Harley-Davidson still headed motorcycle sales in the USA; Indian with the 596cc Scout, 997cc Chief and 1234cc Big Chief, all side-valve V-twins, and the 348cc single-cylinder Prince. All models were also popular in Europe and Australia. Harley-Davidson built a 348cc sv and ohv single cylinder model in 1926.

The 144cc Austro-Motorette, from the drawing-board of Karl Schüber, was a technically-interesting vertical twin two-stroke machine, made in Austria. Puch added to the 123cc model a 174cc double-piston two-stroke and DSH built a whole range with Villiers and JAP engines. Dunelt now had a 248cc version of the double-diameter piston engine, while FN added a 497cc ohv single to the already existing 347cc ohv single and the big 748cc air-cooled four-in-line. Husqvarna built 548cc and 992cc V-twins with their own sv engines. James had small V-twins with 496cc sv and ohv engines in its wide range.

Equipped with ioe engines, NSU of Germany also had V-twins from 498cc to 996cc and Jock Porter, manufacturer and rider from Edinburgh, still supplied his Blackburne-engined New Gerrards, which brought him many racing successes. A one-model range was introduced by Rudge-Whitworth Ltd. in Coventry. It was a

THE ENGINES OF THE TWENTIES

Make	Bore:	Stroke:	Cubic Capacity:	Cyl
Alcyon	62	56	174	TS 1
Blackburne	53	79	174	sv 1
	56.2	79	196	sv 1
	63	79	246	sv 1
	69	79	295	sv 1
	69	92	345	sv 1
	81	96.8	498	sv 1
	85	105	598	sv 1
	50	88	173	ohv 1
	56.2	79	196	ohv 1
	60	88	248	ohv 1
	71	88	348	ohv 1
	71	88	348	ohv 1
	71	88	348	ohv 1
	81	96.8	496	ohv 1
	81	96.8	496	ohv 1
	81	96.8	496	ohv 1
	85	105	598	ohv 1
BMW	68	68	493	sv 2
Bradshaw	68	96	349	ohv 1
Coventry-Victor	63	78	499	ohv 2
	69	78	596	sv 2
	75	78	688	sv 2
	78	78	749	ohv 2
DKW	64	64	206	TS 1
	68	68	246	TS 1
Hanfland JAP	55	65	149	TS 1
	60	62	174	sv 1
	55	83	197	sv 1
	64.5	76	248	sv 1
	70	78	299	sv 1
	70	90	345	sv 1
	85.7	85	490	sv 1
	85.7	104	599	sv 1
	70	88	674	sv 2
	70	97	746	sv 2
	85.7	85	976	sv 2
	85.7	85	976	sv 2
	85.7	85	976	sv 2
	53	78	174	ohv 1
	62.5	80	248	ohv 1
	70	90	348	ohv 1
	85.7	85	490	ohv 1
	85.7	104	599	ohv 1
JAP	70	88	674	ohv 2
	74	85	731	ohv 2
	85.7	85	981	ohv 2
Küchen	70	90	346	sv 1
('K')	79	100	490	sv 1
	70	90	346	ohc 1
	79	100	490	ohc 1
Kühne (Bark)	72	84	342	ohv 1
	84	90	498	sv 1
	84	90	498	ohv 1
MAG (Moto sacoche)	64	77	248	ioe 1
	72	85	346	ioe 1
	82	94	496	ioe 1
	64	77	496	ioe 2
	72	91	741	ioe 2
	82	94	996	ioe 2
	82	103.5	1094	ioe 2
	64	77	248	ohv 1
	72	85	346	ohv 1
	82	94	496	ohv 1
Moser	56	50	124	ohv 1
	60	61	172	ohv 1
Norman Villiers	60	60	170	ohv 1
	50	62	122	TS 1
	55	62	147	TS 1
	57.15	67	172	TS 1
	57.15	67	172	TS 1
	61	67	196	TS 1
	67	70	247	TS 1
	79	70	342	TS 1
Vulpine	78	104	498	ohv 1
	78	104	996	ohv 2

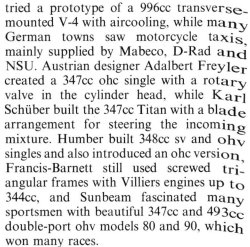

498cc four-valve, four-speed ohv single with coupled brakes. Wanderer in Germany had four-valve cylinders too; one model used a V-twin of 708cc and had therefore a total of 8 valves. They also built a flat 196cc single with 4 valves.

A 498cc ohv AJS single, the Douglas sv models — horizontal twins — and a heavy 496cc single-cylinder unit-design D-Rad were among the new creations of 1926. Another was the 498cc V-twin Blackburne ohv racing engine, used in the Senior TT, by Wal Handley and Jock Porter. It was quite fast, but had a tendency to overheat and never went into quantity production. A similar fate befell the MAG ohv V-twins of 498cc and 598cc, as well as works racing V-twins with 748cc. They could be used in short distance events, but overheated in long road races.

Many designers devoted much time and expense to new two-stroke machines. Among them was the Austrian Anton Gazda, who built 248cc motorcycles but became well-known for his Gazda handlebars, consisting of a bundle of leaf springs. An interesting design was the Paramount-Duo, because of its long wheelbase, two very low bucket seats and an enclosed engine supplied by JAP. It was shown at Olympia in London, but was never built in quantity. The Czechoslovakian Böhmerland also had a very long wheelbase and many other interesting technical details. The engine in this case was a 598cc ohv single, designed by Böhmerland boss Albin

Liebisch. Villiers built a 344cc vertical-twin proprietary two-stroke for the first time, but after a short period it was dropped. A few machines using it were made by Francis-Barnett in England, NSH in Germany, MT in Austria, La Mondiale in Belgium and Monet-Goyon in France.

1927 brought the opening of the Nürburgring, the first 'Cammy' AJS and also the first ohc 490cc Norton, designed by Walter Moore. Indian bought the ACE four, Dougal Marchant joined Motosacoche as designer, and Granville Bradshaw, creator of the ABC, designed the similarly unlucky 247cc Panthette with a transverse-mounted V-twin. Europe's only production version of a 996cc ohc V-twin was a French Koehler-Escoffier, while Windhoff in Germany — where they already built 122cc and 172cc watercooled two-strokes — entered the market with a unique oilcooled 748cc four-cylinder machine with shaft drive. George Brough

tried a prototype of a 996cc transverse-mounted V-4 with aircooling, while many German towns saw motorcycle taxis, mainly supplied by Mabeco, D-Rad and NSU. Austrian designer Adalbert Freyler created a 347cc ohc single with a rotary valve in the cylinder head, while Karl Schüber built the 347cc Titan with a blade arrangement for steering the incoming mixture. Humber built 348cc sv and ohv singles and also introduced an ohc version, Francis-Barnett still used screwed triangular frames with Villiers engines up to 344cc, and Sunbeam fascinated many sportsmen with beautiful 347cc and 493cc double-port ohv models 80 and 90, which won many races.

BSA had a 174cc two-stroke in 1927, Douglas a new 347cc ohv horizontally-opposed twin and there was also a Villiers-engined 172cc NUT, while AKD (Abingdon King Dick) now built 173cc singles with their own ohv engines. There were many factories which switched to saddle tanks, including Ariel, the English Excelsior, Raleigh, New Hudson, James, P&M-Panther, Sun, Coventry-Eagle, Dunelt, Royal-Enfield, Zenith and others. New was the DKW-like 490cc W&G with a nearly vertical twin-cylinder two-stroke engine, but while DKW built this type of machine until the Second World War, the British make soon disappeared.

'Lawrence of Arabia' acquired his fifth Brough-Superior in 1928, FN in Belgium now built 497cc ohv singles, while another Belgian make, Gillet Herstal, had the 348cc Tour de Monde two-stroke single, as well as 498cc ohv singles with their own unit-design engines, and 998cc V-twins with MAG-built ioe engines. In America, the combination of ACE and Indian led to the aircooled 1265cc four-in-line Indian ACE. AJS added a 498cc ohc model to the existing 347cc version of the chain-driven Cammy and Rush, the Belgian make, now built 345cc and 495cc sv and ohv models with their own engines. Moto-Guzzi showed at Milan a spring frame with a 497cc ohv engine and Della Ferrera (not to be confused with Frera) had a new 173cc unit-design ohv model. There was a beautiful production version of the 348cc ohc Bianchi with double ports. And while many experts regarded the English Sunbeam as the non-plus-ultra in motorcycling, it was the Swiss Motosacoche which had this dis-

A rocket-powered motorcycle was tested by Fritz von Opel in 1928. The machine was basically a 496cc Opel Motoclub ohv production model with rockets strapped to the rear end. Soon after this short-lived experiment, Opel stopped making motorcycles.

tinction on the Continent. A new German make, Standard, came very near to Motosacoche as far as quality and finish were concerned.

America had in contrast to Europe only few makes left in 1928: Harley-Davidson, Indian, Super-X, Henderson and Cleveland. DKW was the leading make in Europe. Japan imported machines from England and the USA; their own production was on a very limited scale. The French DFR had a car-type ball gearchange in its four-speed box. The German Neander had a frame made from Duralumin, the BMW new 739cc sv and ohv flat twins, as well as new frames made from pressed steel. BMW works racers got supercharged twins for the 500cc and 750cc classes and Puch of Austria had a new 248cc double-piston two-stroke designed by Giovanni Marcellino. Sturmey-Archer, famous for gearboxes, entered the field with proprietary four-stroke engines from 173cc to 597cc, including a 248cc face-cam ohc version, fitted by Dunelt. Italian factories now built 174cc ohv and ohc models; these included Benelli, Miller, Augusta, Ladetto & Blatto, FVL, Gazzi, Giacomasso, Piana and others.

George William Patchett, ex-McEvoy designer, joined FN and two years later Jawa. Dougal Marchant created very fast 348cc and 498cc ohc racing machines for Motosacoche, with which Walter Handley won the GP of Europe in both classes. England saw the unorthodox Cyril Pullin-designed Ascot-Pullin with a horizontal 497cc ohv single-cylinder engine and OEC introduced duplex steering.

A Rocket-driven Opel motorcycle was tested by Fritz von Opel in Germany, and with Speedway racing coming from Australia to Britain, many factories there — including Douglas, Rudge, Sunbeam, Norton, BSA, James, Calthorpe, Zenith, etc. — built special machines for the sport. Even Scott had such a model. Harley-Davidson came to Europe with such machines, which became known as 'peashooters'.

A new motorcycle factory entered the market in 1929: Jawa of Czechoslovakia. The first model was built under German Wanderer licence. It had a 497cc single-cylinder unit-design ohv engine, a pressed-steel frame and shaft drive. Puch built the first watercooled 248cc works racing two-strokes with double-piston engines and a piston-pump in the crankcase.

Among works machines at Brooklands, Bert Denly rode a 743cc single-cylinder ohc AJS and Bert le Vack a 665cc ohv New Hudson. Germany produced in 1929 195,686 motorcycles, England 164,000. Spanish makes did not appear abroad until after WWII. There was quite a big production in Belgium, with FN, Saroléa, Gillet-Herstal, Rush, La Mondiale, Lady, Ready and a few smaller producers. New in 1929 was a 497cc Harley-Davidson sv single, a 996cc René-Gillet sv V-twin from France and Gillet-Herstal broke 32 world records with the Van Oirbeck-designed 498cc ohc machine. The factory never sold ohc machines and tried everything to hide them from photographers. Even when they had a model called the Record in the catalogue, it had an ohv engine.

We had overhead camshaft engines — like the Velocette, Norton, Chater Lea, AJS — mainly for racing, but other factories including Praga, Chaise, Matchless, Soyer, Dollar etc. also built such power-units in sports models or even touring machines. And when Bert Le Vack broke the world record on August 25, 1929 with 129 mph (208 km/h), his JAP racing V-twin 55 hp engine in its Brough-Superior frame also had overhead valves. New was the five-country Trial in the centre of Europe, but there was a debacle at the International Six-Day Trial, because of the very bad organisation.

Motosacoche's chief designer Dougal Marchant created a new 248cc single-cylinder ohc racing machine with 27 hp running on alcohol, which was then permitted in road races. 27 hp was for 1929 a superb output by a two-fifty. Interesting also were the four-port 498cc ohv NUT, the 247cc six-port Levis two-stroke, the 494cc watercooled vertical-twin DKW two-strokes, Terrot's square cylinders on the 173cc two-strokes, Sunbeams new saddle tanks, the 493cc ohv Slopers made by BSA and the big 998cc JAP and partly Anzani-engined ohv V-twins produced by Brough-Superior, AJW, Delta-Gnom, Tornax, Ardie, Bücker, Standard, Zenith, OEC and others.

1929 was the year when a 498cc ohv Sunbeam (ridden by Charlie Dodson) won for the last time a Senior TT race and when a 172cc Villiers engine of the Brooklands type in a James frame won the 175cc class in the Belgian Grand Prix, with Bert Kershaw riding. Harley-Davidson introduced a new 746cc sv V-twin, Premier in Czechoslovakia a 498cc long-stroke ohv single and Motobécane of France built a 498cc air-cooled four-in-line.

With the dawn of a new decade, so the era of the entrepreneur-engineer was ending. It had been a golden age.

THE SECOND WORLD WAR

THE MOTORCYCLE saw considerable service in both of the two world wars, but its duties on each occasion were rather different. In the First World War, it had been frequently used by the infantry; in World War Two, it was seen first and foremost as a vehicle of communications, particularly by the Allies. Thus the dispatch rider became one of the war's heroic figures.

About 300,000 American motorcycles were built for World War Two. The bikes were all V-twins. One model, the 500cc Indian, was especially designed for the European war, but this bike was low in power and high in weight. The 750cc Harley 45, on the other hand, was a considerable success. With a top speed of more than 85mph from its racing-trained engine, and the ability to cruise for long distances at high speeds, it out-performed its European contemporaries in road work. It was also successful in the North African campaigns.

The Harley-Davidson company had produced bikes in Japan under the name of Rikuo before the war, then the plant was taken over by the state. Although the Eastern theatres of war rarely had the right terrain for motorcycles, the Japanese Army was equipped with these 'Rikuo' Harleys and they were even used by the Emperor's escort.

The British military motorcycles were mainly medium-weight, 350 singles, with top speeds of little more than 70 mph, capable of good performances both on the road and across country. The Matchless G3L was one of the most popular, with the Ariel NH and the Triumph HRW close behind. Then came the AJS R7, the forerunner of the marque's post-war Grand Prix machine.

The Willys-Ford Jeep did much of the general purpose work which the Axis powers consigned to motorcycle variations. One of the more bizarre among such variations was the tracked motorcycle. This creature was exemplified by the excessively heavy German 'Kettenkrad', made by NSU and powered by a 1·5 litre Opel engine.

A simpler and more effective approach was found in the development of motorcycle combinations with sidecar-wheel drive. The Belgian FN factory launched a 1,000cc flat-twin series, the M12, in 1934 for Service use. This was essentially a tricycle, driving on the two rear wheels, which could be fitted with a differential gear. FN chose to drop the tricycle layout in favour of a conventional combination when they produced a heavily-armoured version, the M86, in which the sidecar wheel was driven but had no differential. The usefulness of this machine was destroyed by its great and badly distributed weight.

The Germans took over the FN factory once they occupied Belgium. In France, they were also impressed by the Gnome-Rhône combination, which had sidecar-wheel drive but no differential. When the German Forces needed a new outfit to replace the BMW R12 motorcycle combination, the FN and Gnome & Rhône combinations were available for study, and the project was given to BMW and Zündapp. The resulting BMW R75 with an overhead-valve engine could reach 55 mph with a three-man crew and full loading, and had remarkable off-road performance, only exceeded by the new Zündapp KS.

Zündapp then introduced the differential gear, which was unique on a conventional combination. The gear did not split power equally between the two driving wheels, but shared torque according to the centre of gravity between them. BMW shared this system, along with numerous other components, such as electrical and carburation equipment. These outfits were very effective, though they were costly and complicated to build and could not be manufactured quickly enough.

The Italians placed their faith in the solo machine with a classic Moto-Guzzi, the Alce, the forerunner of today's uprated Falconi. The Alce was a beautifully designed bike: its top speed was 80 mph, and the forward facing horizontal layout of its 500cc engine contributed to a weight distribution which helped stability and manoeuvrability. An Alce was produced with a machine-gun mounted on the handlebars, and an additional pair of dummy handlebars for the pillion passenger to support the bike while the driver used the gun. Alternatively the pillion passenger could lean over and fire the gun while the driver supported the bike. Predictably neither of these methods proved very

Military requirements led to a variety of special design. The U.S. Army used Harley-Davidson 45 WLAs (facing page) with a holster for a submachine gun. The British experimented with attachments for a mortar and a submachine gun (big picture) on Norton motorcycles. The Germans tried a scooter for paratroops, and a tracked vehicle, the NSU HK101 Kettenkrad.

practicable for safe and effective use.

Gilera manufactured a 500cc single, which was notable for the use of both side and over-head valves within the same engine, and Bianchi and Sertim produced more conventional side-valve 500cc models. All three were frequently fitted with side-cars.

As the portability, reliability and range of radio improved, and other means of communication developed, the military usefulness of the motorcycle faded from immediate view. Nor in the post-war period would motorcycling ever quite recover its former colour, though the British Corgi and American Cushman 'parascooters' briefly brought a minuscule new dimension to two-wheel riding, and the Piaggi aircraft company developed the Vespa scooter.

Many different manufacturers supplied machines for military use. American M.P.s used the Harley-Davidson; BMW supplied their R35 (below) and R75 (right). Bottom: BSA were one of the major British suppliers, making both 350 and 500cc models. The Indian soldier is reclining on a Matchless G3/L, a 350cc ohv machine.

THE GREAT DESIGNERS

The most famous and successful motorcycles have been designs so good that they have been produced for many years with a minimum of modernization and development.

Adalberto Garelli designed his first double-piston two-strokes before 1914; they continued to be developed until 1935. J. L. Norton designed the Norton sv singles which won so many races; as a normal production version, the 16H was in the catalogue for many years and was made in thousands for the military during the Second World War. The Austrian Puch machines had a very long run; designed by Giovanni Marcellino in 1923, they were made until the 1960s. Marcellino's masterpieces were works racing machines having 248cc watercooled engines with pumping pistons in the crankcase. At the German Grand Prix in 1931, they beat everything in sight. Not all designers stayed with one

company. Edward Turner had joined Ariel in 1927; his 1930 Ariel square four was a big success. In 1936 he took over Triumph on behalf of its new owner, Jack Sangster; the next year he built Triumph's first 498cc vertical twin, the Speed Twin, by fitting the engine into an existing frame from a single-cylinder model. It was an instant success. There had been two previous Triumph vertical twins: a 448cc prototype in 1913, and a 649cc ohv unit-design model designed by Val Page in 1933, which was marketed at a time when few buyers could afford such a big machine. Page was a very good designer who had worked for years on JAP proprietary engines, but the 1937 Triumph vertical twin was a perfect example of the right design at the right time; it was the first commercially successful vertical twin, and inspired a great many others.

Famous designer George William Pat-

chett joined Jawa in Prague, after being with George Brough, Michael McEvoy and the FN works. His designs for Jawa included two machines—a 173cc and a 246cc two-stroke with pressed steel frames, and 346cc sv and ohv singles. There were also 247cc two-strokes with Auto-Union (Schnürle patent) flat-top engines.

Harold Willis designed the Roarer for Velocette in 1939; this was a supercharged vertical twin ohc with 498cc and shaft drive. The war and Willis's death prevented racing of the machine. After the war, Charles Udall was responsible for the silent watercooled Velocette LE, with a 198cc transverse-mounted flat twin, in connection with Percy and Bertie Goodmann.

In the 1920s Richard Küchen designed the famous 3-valve 'K' series of proprietary engines; in the 1930s, he was responsible

The famous British designer Bradshaw began his career with the ABC in 1913

Marcellino (centre) designed two-cylinder, four-piston 246cc Puch racing two-strokes.

Norton genius O'Donovan and passenger Rex Judd.

Creator of the Speed Twin . . . Edward Turner (standing directly behind the fuel tank)

George William Patchett (left) of McEvoy, FN and Jawa and Walter William Moore of Douglas, Norton and NSU.

for sv and ohv engines as well. In 1933, he created the Zündapp range, with pressed steel frames and two and four-stroke engines from 198 to 798cc. The biggest was a transverse-mounted flat four, and many models had shaft drive. After the Second World War, Küchen designed Opti vertical twin ohc proprietary engines, double-piston two-strokes and even racing car engines. His engines were always of clean design, but their finesse was often the work of his lesser-known brother, Xaver.

Between the wars, George Brough continued to construct the most expensive motorcycles in the world, but he never built his own engines, using MAG, JAP and Matchless units. In 1932 be built 796cc models with two rear wheels, and they had watercooled Austin car engines. Some prototypes had engine parts made by Motosacoche; among these was the Dream, with a 996cc transverse-mounted flat-four.

An outstanding design of 1935 was the AJS 499cc double-ohc V-four, which was the work of Bert Collier. It was afterwards modified to watercooling and also supercharged in 1939, and was the fastest pre-war British road racer of its size.

W. W. Moore had designed the first Norton ohc machine in 1927. In 1930 he joined the German NSU works and created the not dissimilar 490cc single. His work at Norton was taken over by Arthur Carroll, while Irishman Joe Craig took over development and team management. Carroll redesigned the camshaft arrangement and made the Nortons faster and more reliable before his death in an accident in 1935. (From 1950 onwards, Norton machines had the superb featherbed frame, the Irish invention of Rex and Crommie McCandless and Artie Bell.)

After World War II, German Victoria had the 198cc 'Swing', a swinging arm two-

stroke designed by Norbert Riedel. In 1948 Riedel designed the very unorthodox Imme, a 98cc two-stroke with a one-sided fork and the engine on the swinging arm. Sunbeams designed after the war by Ealing Poppe were entirely different machines from the pre-war models, with 498cc vertical-twin ohc in-line engines and shaft drive. Vincenz Sklenar designed 348 and 498cc double-ohc racing twins right after the war; Jaroslav Walter created 248 and 348cc ohc singles for CZ after 1949. When MV-Agusta entered racing in the early 1950s, the 498cc four was designed by Piero Remor.

Among today's designers, primarily two-stroke specialists, are such great names as Dr. Kippitsch, Muller, Thiel, Van Veen, Bianchi, Larsson, Hooper, Dyson, Feri, J. Möller, Kameyama, Magni, Tominaga, Taglioni, Nakano, Zen and Semba, to name just a few.

Crommie McCandless ... of featherbed fame

Remor (left) with Gilera

Val Page of JAP, Ariel and Triumph.

Fabio Taglioni (above) designed the Ducati desmodromic valve gear in the early 1960s. The system is still in use. Right: Giulio Carcano with Moto-Guzzi Junior TT winner in 1956.

Jack Williams, chief development engineer on the AJS 7R, with son-in-law Tom Herron, of Yamaha

Pioneer Max Friz ... he made aircraft engines, then the first BMW motorcycle

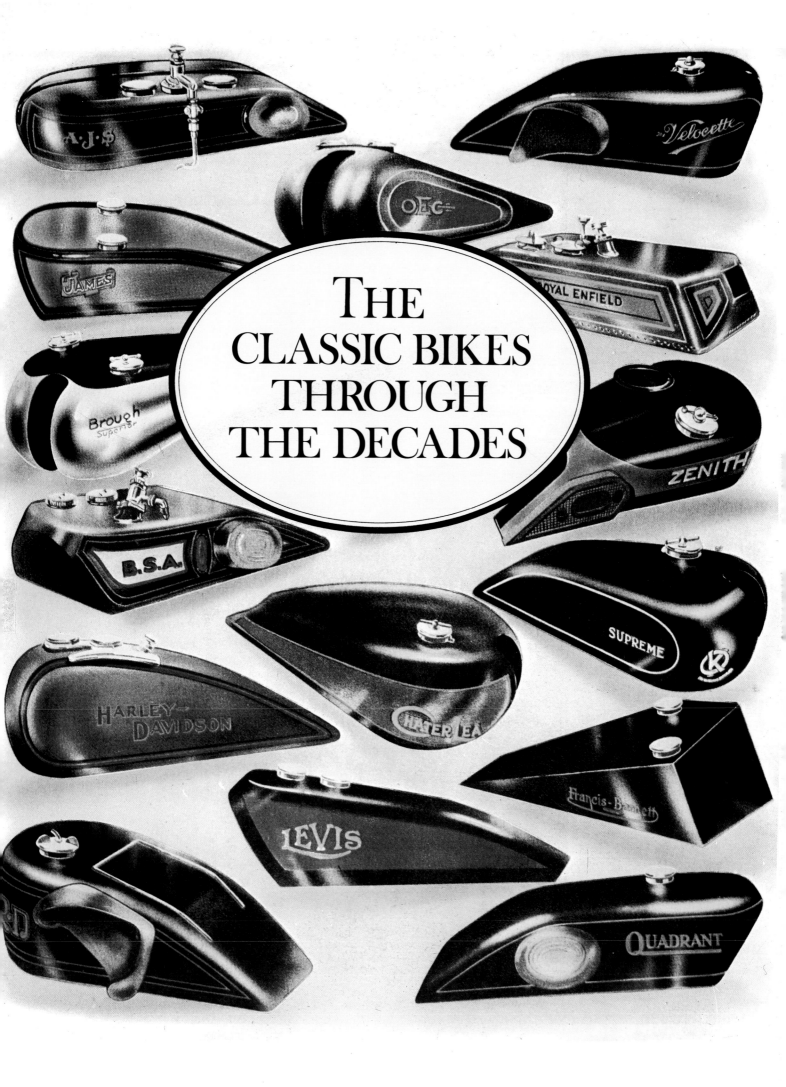

THE CLASSIC BIKES THROUGH THE DECADES

NO FOUR-CYLINDER MOTORCYCLE has achieved such pre-eminence in its own time as the Henderson. It provided riders in the early years of motorcycling with simple starting, smoothness, silence, oil tightness, reliability and generous power to a degree unmatched elsewhere. The model shown here is that of 1912, the first year of production. The original 7 hp model was soon further developed, with a multi-speed gearbox, improved power, and more robust construction. Sales rose accordingly, and the model achieved greater popularity than any comparable machine in the United States. Finally, Ignaz Schwinn's Excelsior Company bought the firm in 1917, initially retaining the services of founders William and Tom

Henderson. After that, the Henderson big four also incorporated the name Excelsior on the tank. Two years later, William and Tom Henderson left Excelsior, unhappy with the new business arrangement. William founded his own motorcycle company, under the name of Ace. He was soon manufacturing an Ace four, and challenging the Henderson's reputation for quality. After many successful years Ace ran into financial troubles, and was bought by Indian.

THE NAME SCOTT is central to the history of the motorcycle. Alfred Scott was an inventor and engine-designer who played a leading part in the development of the two-stroke machine. Scott built his first motorised bicycle in Yorkshire as early as 1898, using a twin-cylinder two-stroke. The engine was fitted to a heavy pedal-cycle, and transmission was by friction roller. By 1903, he had built a machine with rear-wheel power, and a year later Scott was granted British patent rights on a two-stroke vertical-twin engine. Scott's first true production motorcycle was manufactured in 1908. Its engine was built to the Scott design by the nearby Jowett car factory, another Yorkshire concern famous in automotive history. This 333cc engine had a bore and stroke of 58 × 63mm, and the entire unit weighed only 371 lbs. The cylinder heads were water-cooled through a thermosiphon system, but the barrels were air-cooled. By 1914, Scott had settled the design of his machines, and was using a wholly water-cooled engine. The two-speed machine had standard gear-ratios of 3:1 and 4:1, and the unusual "open" frame design which characterised the marque. This frame design was popular with women motorcyclists, whose dignity it helped preserve. Telescopic front forks were used from the very first, and a disc-valve induction and exhaust system was introduced at an early stage. Other machines could match the Scott's 55 mph top speed, but none of its contemporaries offered the same handling qualities. It was this characteristic in particular which afforded Scott such great racing success. Like most unconventional machines, the Scott was the creature of its designer. Alfred Scott himself left the company after the First World War, and died in 1923; within four or five years, the marque had lost much of its shine. Production since a takeover in 1950 has been limited to small-scale revivals. The Scott shown here is a 486cc model specially reconstructed for vintage racing.

INDIAN WAS WITHOUT DOUBT one of the foremost names in the development of the modern motorcycle. In 1905, the factory became one of the first to put a V-twin into commercial manufacture. The first V engine was little more than a doubling up of two Indian 1·75 hp singles, but improved and enlarged versions soon followed. These ultimately provided the basis for the very advanced motorcycles produced under the aegis of the factory's founder, George Hendee, and the great designer Oskar Hedström. After they had left the company, Charlie Gustafson became Indian's chief designer in 1915. He established the side-valve style which became a tradition of the factory and of the American motorcycle industry. His great machine

was the 7 hp 998 cc Power Plus shown here. This sophisticated and speedy motorcycle included such advanced equipment as leaf-spring suspended pivoted fork rear suspension, all chain drive, electric lighting, electric starting and a proper kick-start.

Indian

CLASSIC BIKES

AS THE ORIGINAL William Brough motor-cycle company entered the last year of its life, the son's rival firm launched the most famous machine to bear the family name. The Brough Superior SS100, introduced in 1925 was more popular than any other prestige sports roadster before or since. The SS100, shown here, was an overhead-valve V-twin. It became one of the two mainstays of Brough Superior's 19-year production period, along with its predecessor, the SS80 side-valve V-twin. As with all engines of its type, the side-valve twin was less durable at speed than the ohv. The '100' and '80' model designations referred to the machines' guaranteed top speed. Brough Superior was also known for a proliferation of multi-cylindered exotica.

Brough Superior

The machines were largely assembled from proprietary components — the engines were principally JAP or Matchless units, and even the famous Castle forks were originally a Harley Davidson design. This philosophy was the Achilles' heel of Brough Superior.

The company tried unsuccessfully to develop its own power-units, and the cost of buying-in specially-manufactured engines in small quantities eventually proved to be crippling. The company stopped motorcycle production in 1940.

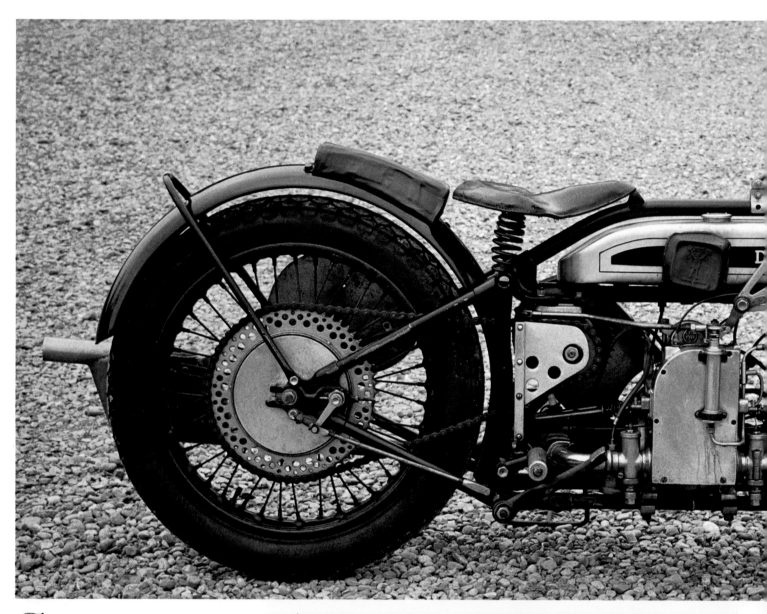

SUNBEAM

THE SUNBEAM MODEL 90, shown on the right in its traditional black-and-gold livery, is probably the finest example of British single-cylinder engineering. It used simple, proven designs, with meticulous finish. The machine was conceived in 1923 as a sports roadster, and successfully adapted as a works racer. It was produced in both 350 and 500cc ohv versions. Production standards dropped after the factory was bought in 1930 by ICI (Imperial Chemical Industries). Sunbeam was later owned by Associated Motorcycles and BSA.

Douglas

ALTHOUGH DOUGLAS did sometimes use other engine layouts, the marque was always known for its horizontally-opposed twins. Today, Douglas is usually remembered for its post-war series of transverse-engined 350cc machines, but these were only made in the company's last seven years. In its earlier days, and for more than three decades, Douglas found its fame and fortune in exceptionally well-planned twins with a fore-and-aft arrangement. The success of these machines owed much to the work of the company's chief development rider, Freddie Dixon, during the middle and late 1920s. Fate also played a part. When the Douglas EW series of 350sv racers began to find the competition tough, Douglas had planned a new ohc model, but a fire at the works destroyed the blueprints and set back the company's work. The new engine was abandoned, and the company chose instead to give a new life to its old ohv twins, with considerable development work by Dixon. By happy chance, these machines proved most successful in the newly-arrived sport of speedway. Some of their success was due to a freak of design which led the frame to flex during broadsliding, but their achievements on the cinder track boosted all aspects of the Douglas reputation. During this period, the classic Douglas machine was the model FW, which was produced in 500cc and 600cc versions. The road-racing version is shown here. The road-racing models were capable of 90 mph and 95 mph respectively. In 1929 alone, 1300 machines were sold.

Rudge

SOME OF THE BEST British production bikes were replicas of their makers' works racing models. A fine example was the 1929 Rudge-Whitworth Ulster, which came from a factory famous for its advanced approach. The machine was introduced to celebrate Graham Walker's win in the Ulster Grand Prix, and it proved to be exceptionally fast and reliable. It had a four-speed positive-stop, foot-change gearbox, dry sump lubrication with a mechanical pump, and a four-valve cylinder head in a penthouse combustion chamber.

171

THE BRITISH EXCELSIOR company is remembered with affection for a 250cc
single which was popularly known as the
"Mechanical Marvel," but this four-valve
ohv machine suffered from its own com-
plexity. Undaunted, Excelsior continued
along the same development path with
an improved four-valver, the famous
Manxman, shown here. This machine had
a single overhead camshaft, and each
inlet valve was fed by its own Amal RN
carburettor. The bronze head, as shown,
improved thermal efficiency in the days
before aluminium had come into common
use. The Manxman shown is a 250, but a
350 was also produced. Valve gear and
carburettor tune still proved "very
pernickerty" according to Excelsior's
managing director Eric Walker, and in
1938 the firm introduced two-valve engines.
These were equally fast, but wholly reliable.
They had sprung frames, and proved so
successful that they continued to be raced
in private hands into the early 1950s.

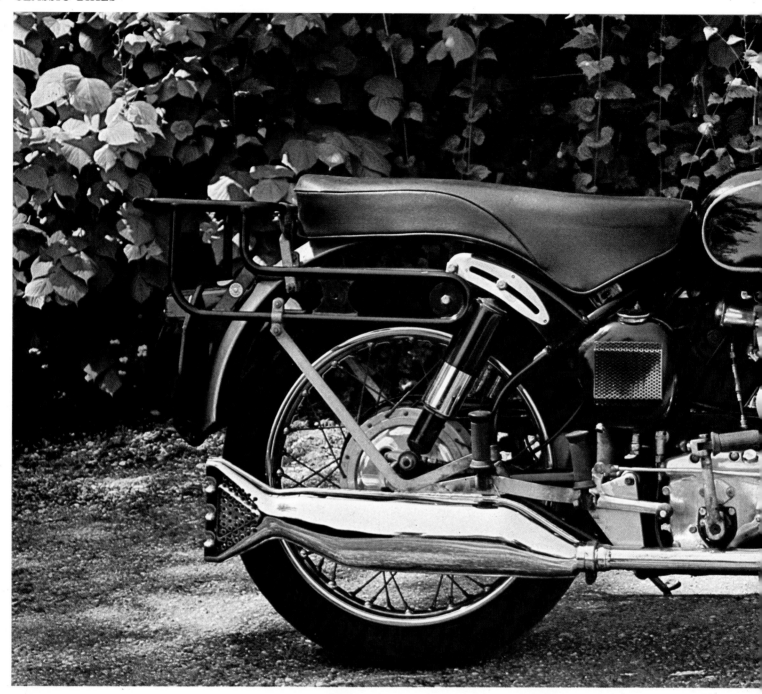

Velocette

OTHER SINGLE-CYLINDER machines may have exemplified a particular aspect of engineering or of performance, but those produced by Velocette demonstrated the full range of attributes. This was best accomplished by the KTT (left), a racing replica of the works' own grand prix machinery, which was also notable as the first model to sport the Velocette-perfected foot gear-change system. This was an ohc

single of 350cc, sold with a guaranteed top speed of 85 mph. As an option, Velocette offered a 100 mph dope-tuned model sporting a 9:1 compression ratio. The range ran from the 1929 Mk 1 illustrated here to the 1949 Mk VIII. In 1956, Velocette demonstrated its skills with a quite different range of well-remembered singles. These were ohv sports roadsters. First came the 499cc Venom, shown above, with a "square" (86 × 86mm) engine, then the smaller 349cc Viper. The Venom engine developed 36 bhp at 6,200 rpm, giving the machine a top speed of 95 mph. After 12 and 24-hour records had been set at Montlhéry, a highly-tuned version was produced as a clubman racer. This was the Thruxton (right), which had a top speed of approximately 120 mph.

BSA

FOR MOST OF ITS LIFE, the BSA marque was known primarily for singles of simple and inexpensive design, made for everyday transport. The motorcycles in the small picture are examples: a 250cc machine from 1925 (background) and the 1928 "Sloper". In later years, the same qualities of durability and reliability were showcased in a much more exotic motorcycle, the Gold Star. No clubman racer has ever enjoyed the success or reputation of the "Goldie". The range was produced in trial, scramble, touring and racing versions, and a 1959 model of the latter is shown here. The 500cc engine developed up to 40 bhp at just over 7,000 rpm, through a close ratio gearbox. Top speed was around 120 mph in full clubman trim.

88751

HARLEY–DAVIDSON

THE HARLEY-DAVIDSON Electra-Glide has its origins in the SV 74 twin of 1922, although its more recent and direct ancestor is the first ohv 1200 of 1941. These early machines displayed the familiar styling features of most American motorcycles: leading link front forks, solid rear wheel mounting, pan saddles, footboards, high, wide handle-bars, and a V-twin engine, all of which produce comfort at low cruising speeds. Over the years, the range has been modernised and renamed, but the essential concept has remained the same. In 1949, the Hydra-Glide was introduced with a telescopic front fork. The next model, with pivoted-fork rear suspension, produced in 1959, was the Duo-Glide. With the addition of a starter motor in 1965 came the name Electra-Glide. Since then, little has changed except the adoption of cast alloy wheels, although numerous Japanese components, such as forks and carburettor, have been adopted. The Electra-Glide is the heaviest mass-produced motorcycle ever built, weighing 800 lbs fully equipped. The 45°, 1207cc V-twin has hydraulically-activated push-rods and produces 62 bhp at 5,200 rpm, and 70ft/lbs of torque at 4,000 rpm. For all its cumbrous luxury, the Harley has a speedy history. In the 1920s, when the marque was locked in competition with Indian, sporting feats were constantly being publicised. In 1920, several new times were set over a kilometre at Daytona. Harley, which was already well known in Britain, also made several celebrated runs at Brooklands. The 1,200cc machine shown below broke the Flying Kilometre record in 1923, at 108·6 mph, in the hands of the famous British rider Freddie Dixon.

THERE ARE MANY REASONS for celebrating the famous marque founded by Howard R. Davies (hence its original name, HRD) and bought shortly afterwards by Philip Vincent. Modern motorcycle manufacturers have still barely caught up with the progressive chassis-group designs produced by Vincent 35 years ago, though the marque is more commonly remembered for its spree of speedy achievement during the 1950s. Perhaps these sporting feats were the inspiration for the unusually-large and ambitious speedo which was fitted to Vincent motorcycles. Factory and private riders captured national and world speed and sprint records by the

handful on the competition model of the period, the Black Lightning. The word "Black" featured in the names of several famous Vincent machines. One unsupercharged Black Lightning achieved a speed of 185·15 mph in the hands of Russell Wright, a New Zealander, in 1955. Sadly, this was also the last year of full production.

The firm went out in a blaze of glory, with the announcement of the semi-streamlined Series D models, but few were actually made. In design, these machines were the natural successors to the Series C Rapides, which had been launched in 1949, with 50-degree 998cc V-twin engines. The Series C standard touring machine provided a top speed of approximately 105/110 mph, and its sporting counterpart the Black Shadow (shown here) went to 110/120 mph, reaching 56 mph in only six seconds. These machines were in turn developed from the Series A Rapides, which were launched in 1937, had 47-degree engines, and had a web of external pipes.

ARIEL was in every sense an historic British marque. Established since 1898, the firm exhibited all the characteristics of British motorcycle manufacture. The products were well made, even sporty, but initially of conventional design. In 1929, a much more sophisticated machine made a considerable break with tradition. This was a 500cc four with a highly-unusual "square" cylinder configuration and single overhead camshaft. This distinctive engine layout became so identifiable with the marque that the nickname "Squariel" passed into the language of motorcycling. Like the later Triumph Speed Twin, another pace-setting machine, the Square

Four was designed by Edward Turner. It had an all ball-and-roller bearing engine and horizontally-split crankcase. In 1931, the engine was bored out from 51 to 56 mm, thus increasing capacity to 600cc. Although some modest success was achieved in competition, such as the Bickel

brothers' supercharged 111·42 lap at Brooklands in 1934, the machine was really a sporting tourer. In 1936, Ariel launched a 1,000cc Square Four of quite new engine design. This model had a pushrod power-unit, with plain bearings, and it also utilised a unique trailing-link rear-suspension system. It remained in production in various roadster forms until the late 1950s, by which time it boasted four individual exhaust-pipes ports and an all-aluminium engine. The 1956 luxury roadster shown here develops 42 bhp at 5,800 rpm, providing a top speed of 105 mph. It has a bore and stroke of 65 × 75 mm. The machine's kerb-weight is 495 lbs.

TRIUMPH

TRIUMPH WILL ALWAYS be associated with the vertical-twin engine-layout. This classic design was introduced in 1938, in the 498cc Speed Twin, which was the forerunner of many famous motorcycles. A memorable example was the larger Thunderbird (above), introduced in 1949. This 649cc tourer produced 34 bhp at 6,000 rpm on a compression ratio of 7:1. Three standard models averaged 101·06 mph between them for 500 miles at Montlhéry. A total break with the vertical-twin layout came in the 1960s with the transverse three-cylinder Trident (left). The T160 had a 740cc engine of 67×70 mm bore and stroke, giving 58 bhp at 7,250 rpm to reach a top speed of around 120 mph. Production ended in the mid-1970s.

Norton

IT WAS THE GREAT racing success of the Norton marque which created the need for an improved frame in the 1940s. The need was met by the McCandless brothers' Featherbed frame, which in turn influenced motorcycle design almost everywhere. After being introduced on the Manx racers, the Featherbed frame was modified for road use in the existing 497cc tourer, which became the Dominator in 1952. The example shown above is a Manx built in 1958. Ten years after its launch, the Dominator had grown to 647cc, with a maximum road speed of 112 mph. In 1965, Norton launched the 745cc Atlas, but a more significant development came two years later. The same engine was fitted, with rubber mountings, into a new duplex frame. This new model, the Commando, was subsequently increased in size to 828cc. With a top speed of 120 mph, the Commando (bottom) is the most powerful road-going Norton ever produced.

CLASSIC BIKES

LIKE THE LAMBORGHINI CAR, the equally exotic Laverda is the product of an Italian agricultural engineering group. With its race-bred frame and sleek styling, the 130 mph RGS 1000 (below) is Laverda's flagship. It is derived from the Laverda Jota, which with a top speed of 150 mph verified in independent tests, was the fastest production roadster ever built. The RGS 1000 is powered by a 981cc three-cylinder motor which features 120° crankshaft and gives 80 bhp.

THE MV AGUSTA AMERICA is arguably the finest sports roadster in production, and without doubt a classic among the multi-cylindered big bikes. The entire power-unit is a development of the company's racing 500cc four of the 1950s. MV was the last European marque to dominate the Grand Prix circuits, and retired solely for commercial reasons, but it took several attempts before the factory's sporting experience could be translated into a successful roadster. The 788cc dohc America develops 75 bhp at 8,500 rpm, and its top speed is approximately 135 mph.

MOTO GUZZI

WHILE JAPANESE motorcycles have become increasingly sophisticated, the largest of the Italian manufacturers has responded by offering machines of comparable performance but robust simplicity. The V 850 GT of 1972 typifies Moto Guzzi's approach. The transverse twin turns out 64·5 bhp at a mere 6,500 rpm, providing a top speed of 115 mph. In 1975, the entire range was expanded to include the revolutionary V 1,000, with hydraulic torque converter.

DUCATI

IT WAS BUILT for its high-speed handling, apparently with no other priority in mind, and in this respect the Ducati Desmo 864cc of 1975 has no serious rival. Its top speed is 135 mph, its kerb weight a mere 428 lbs, and it is a remarkably stable motorcycle. The machine also benefits from the efficiency and reliability of the desmodromic valve system. Only Ducati has used this system with total success. The technique was employed to great effect in the 1972 750 SS clubman racer, after being first introduced by the factory's chief engineer, Fabioni Taglioni, in the successful Grand Prix period which was during the late 1950s.

UNLIKE THE JAPANESE, the German BMW company prefers the conservative approach of evolving a proven design. The flat twin concept can be traced back to the 1930s. Only in 1983 are BMW to break with tradition by offering a novel along-the-frame dohc in-line four. The R100RS pictured here has changed little from its introduction in the mid-1970s and is closely related to the popular R60 (inset) of a decade ago. Aerodynamically, the R100RS is very advanced, the result of fairing development in the Pinin Farina wind tunnel in Milan. The fairing cuts down front wheel lift, increasing downward pressure by 17·4 per cent. And lateral stability is improved by 60 per cent. These benefits were achieved by designer Hans Muth, whose background

in car styling taught him how to utilise the wind rather than fighting it. Practicality and simplicity are the keynotes of the engine, a horizontally-opposed 980cc ohv twin which gives 70 bhp at 7,000 rpm. Top speed is around 125 mph; the bike will cover the standing quarter-mile in just over 13 seconds. The cockpit layout is in the sports car idiom, and the rider is even pampered with a voltmeter and an electric clock. Ready for the road, the stylish R100RS weighs just over 500 lbs.

CLASSIC BIKES

IT WAS WITH the racing success of machines like the 1960 Honda 250 four (small picture) that the Japanese motorcycle industry first claimed the attention of the Western world. When the sophisticated Gold Wing was launched in 1974, it met with some scepticism, but its elaborate design soon proved itself. The horizontally-opposed transverse four-cylinder layout makes for smooth running; the water-cooling improves the mechanical silencing and temperature control; shaft-drive affords longevity in the transmission; a low centre of gravity comes from placing the gearbox beneath the engine and the 4·2 gallon tank below the seat nose. The dummy tank neatly and accessibly contains the coolant header tank and most

ancillary electrical components and tools. Unusually in a shaft-driven motorcycle, the countershaft-mounted clutch is a wet multi-plate type. A contra-rotating generator alongside it counteracts the lateral torque effect inherent in 'flat'-engined machines. The latest version, the GL1100DC Deluxe shown here, has an sohc 1085cc motor giving 84 bhp at 7,500 rpm. Top speed is over 120 mph. The Deluxe is a luxury tourer for which matching panniers and top box are also offered.

THE RD350LC IS YAMAHA's no-holds-barred street racer and is probably the last two-stroke of its size as emissions legislation tightens. For this reason it is not on sale in the USA. With its 347cc liquid-cooled twin-cylinder engine giving 47 bhp at 8,500 rpm and its race-developed mono-shock frame, the RD350LC will out-perform many larger machines. More sophisticated is the XJ650 Turbo, only the second production bike to be turbo-charged. Its 653cc dohc four-cylinder engine delivers 85 bhp to give a maximum speed of around 125 mph. The instruments feature computerised monitors for fuel levels and electrics.

⚡ SUZUKI

THE GSX1100E KATANA is a 'superbike' in every sense, with a top speed of 140 mph and a standing quarter-mile time of only 11·6 seconds. Its styling is a striking departure from more conventional lines and percolates right through the larger Suzuki models. The four-cylinder dohc 1075cc engine delivers 110 bhp at 8500 rpm and features Twin Swirl Combustion Chambers to give more efficient fuel usage. A novel anti-dive system is used on the front forks, activated by brake fluid pressure. The GSX1100 is descended from the successful GS750 with which Suzuki entered the four-stroke arena in 1977. Before that, Suzuki produced a brave experiment; the Wankel rotary-engined RE5 (right). Although brilliantly engineered, the RE5 was too thirsty and was a sales flop.

◢◤ Kawasaki

KAWASAKI IS THE FIRST manufacturer to offer fuel-injection in production motorcycles as in the GPz1100 shown here. This gives instant starting in any weather and smooth response throughout the rpm range and requires almost no maintenance. The GPz1100 is Kawasaki's bid to get back to the top of the performance tables. Its four-cylinder dohc 1089cc motor produces close to 110 bhp at 8500 rpm to thrust the bike to almost 140 mph.

The 1000cc Z1-R (right) appeared in the late 1970s as a smartly-styled performance roadster with a 123 mph top speed. Like the GPz1100, it is derived from the legendary 900cc Z1, the machine with which Kawasaki successfully trumped Honda's CB750-4 in 1972.

DATE DUE			
DE 21 8	FE 9 '98		
JAN 6 1994			
Jan 23	AG 3 '98		
MR 24 '88	OC 3		
JY 25 '88	AP 23 02		
AG 10 '88	AP 23 '02		
FE 10 90	MY 15 0		
AP 25 '97	MR 24 09		
DE 4 '91			
FE 16 '93			
JE 18 '93			
DE 2 '93			
OC 11 '94			
FE 2 '95			
SE 28 '95			
JY 1 '96			
OC 10 '96			

DEMCO 38-297